Guide and Reference to the Snakes of Western North America
(North of Mexico) and Hawaii

UNIVERSITY PRESS OF FLORIDA

Florida A&M University, Tallahassee
Florida Atlantic University, Boca Raton
Florida Gulf Coast University, Ft. Myers
Florida International University, Miami
Florida State University, Tallahassee
New College of Florida, Sarasota
University of Central Florida, Orlando
University of Florida, Gainesville
University of North Florida, Jacksonville
University of South Florida, Tampa
University of West Florida, Pensacola

University Press of Florida

Gainesville · Tallahassee · Tampa · Boca Raton

Pensacola · Orlando · Miami · Jacksonville · Ft. Myers · Sarasota

Guide and Reference to the

SNAKES

of Western North America (North of Mexico)
and Hawaii

R. D. BARTLETT AND PATRICIA P. BARTLETT

Library of Congress Cataloging-in-Publication Data
Bartlett, Richard D., 1938–
Guide and reference to the snakes of western North America (north
of Mexico) and Hawaii / R. D. Bartlett and Patricia P. Bartlett.
p. cm.
Includes bibliographical references and index.
ISBN 978-0-8130-3301-3 (alk. paper)
1. Snakes—West (U.S.)—Identification. 2. Snakes—Hawaii—
Identification. I. Bartlett, Patricia Pope, 1949– II. Title.
QL666.O6B3294 2009
597.960978—dc22   2008038640

The University Press of Florida is the scholarly publishing agency
for the State University System of Florida, comprising Florida A&M
University, Florida Atlantic University, Florida Gulf Coast University,
Florida International University, Florida State University, New College
of Florida, University of Central Florida, University of Florida,
University of North Florida, University of South Florida, and
University of West Florida.

University Press of Florida
15 Northwest 15th Street
Gainesville, FL 32611-2079
http://www.upf.com

Contents

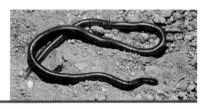

Species

SLENDER BLIND SNAKES, FAMILY LEPTOTYPHLOPIDAE

1. New Mexican Blind Snake, *Leptotyphlops dissectus*
2. Southwestern Blind Snake, *Leptotyphlops humilis humilis*
   3. Desert Blind Snake, *Leptotyphlops humilis cahuilae*
   4. Trans-Pecos Blind Snake, *Leptotyphlops humilis segregus*
   5. Utah Blind Snake, *Leptotyphlops humilis utahensis*

BLIND SNAKES, FAMILY TYPHLOPIDAE

6. Brahminy Blind Snake, *Ramphotyphlops braminus* (mainland and Hawaii)

BOAS, FAMILY BOIDAE

ROSY AND RUBBER BOAS, SUBFAMILY ERICINAE

7. Northern Rubber Boa, *Charina bottae*
8. Southern Rubber Boa, *Charina umbratica*
9. Mexican Rosy Boa, *Lichanura trivirgata trivirgata*
   10. Desert Rosy Boa, *Lichanura trivirgata gracia*
   11. Coastal Rosy Boa, *Lichanura trivirgata roseofusca*

ADVANCED SNAKES I, FAMILY COLUBRIDAE

RACERS, WHIPSNAKES, GREEN SNAKES, RAT SNAKES, KINGSNAKES, GOPHER SNAKES, AND RELATIVES, SUBFAMILY COLUBRINAE

INSECT-EATING SONORINES

SAND SNAKES, SHOVEL-NOSED SNAKES

ADVANCED SNAKES II

COBRAS, CORAL SNAKES, AND RELATIVES, FAMILY ELAPIDAE

CORAL SNAKE, SUBFAMILY MICRURINAE

SEA SNAKES, FAMILY HYDROPHIIDAE

PIT VIPERS, FAMILY VIPERIDAE

RATTLESNAKES, SUBFAMILY CROTALINAE

Quick Reference to the Snakes of Hawaii, Alaska, and Western Canada

HAWAIIAN SNAKES

6. Brahminy Blind Snake, *Ramphotyphlops braminus*
124. Yellow-bellied Sea Snake, *Pelamis platurus*

ALASKAN SNAKES

117. Valley Garter Snake, *Thamnophis sirtalis fitchi*

WESTERN CANADIAN SNAKES

7. Northern Rubber Boa, *Charina bottae*
13. Western Yellow-bellied Racer, *Coluber constrictor mormon*
60. Great Basin Gopher Snake, *Pituophis catenifer deserticola*
62. Bullsnake, *Pituophis catenifer sayi*
78. Sharp-tailed Snake, *Contia tenuis*
88. Northern Desert Night Snake, *Hypsiglena chlorophaea deserticola*
94. Plains Hog-nosed Snake, *Heterodon nasicus*
98a. Northern Red-bellied Snake, *Storeria occipitomaculata occipitomaculata*
106. Wandering Garter Snake, *Thamnophis elegans vagrans*
111. Northwestern Garter Snake, *Thamnophis ordinoides*
113. Plains Garter Snake, *Thamnophis radix*
117. Valley Garter Snake, *Thamnophis sirtalis fitchi*
119. Prairie Red-sided Garter Snake, *Thamnophis sirtalis parietalis*
120. Puget Sound Garter Snake, *Thamnophis sirtalis pickeringii*
139. Northern Pacific Rattlesnake, *Crotalus oreganus oreganus*
144. Prairie Rattlesnake, *Crotalus viridis viridis*

Preface

There is more interest today in the reptiles and amphibians with which we share our world than ever before, and of these creatures, it is the snakes that are foremost in everyone's mind. They may be revered, they may be only tolerated, or they may be detested, but interest exists, and fortunately, tolerance for this important group of animals seems to be increasing. Perhaps the most encouraging thing, is that the interest exists at all levels, from the most basic to the most advanced. Interpretive programs are presented regularly in many grade schools. Programs and assemblies and studies continue through middle school, into high school, and a proliferation of undergraduate and post graduate college courses are now offering insights into our ophidian neighbors.

Besides academic interest, snakes have become popular pet items, the target subjects of ecotours, as well as creatures of interest to gardeners and backyard naturalists. Herpetological clubs, reptile and amphibian expos, and herpetological seminars are found across the country and across the world. Internet chats and online pet forums are readily available to anyone with Internet access. Accurate information about the private lives of many of the more popular snake species is now available to anyone who wishes to have it.

In these pages we have provided information about not only the popular snakes of the American west, but also all snakes from that region—from the tiniest burrower, to the big constricting gopher snakes, to venomous species that seek safe haven in remote mountain fastnesses. We find all 147 species and subspecies to be of immense interest, and sincerely hope we have answered your questions successfully.

1

Introduction

Though large segments of the United States are despoiled, it remains a wonderful country, boasting varied topography, varied climate, myriad environments, and—despite seriously fragmented habitats—a wonderfully diverse fauna.

The topographical variations in the American west are remarkable in many ways. There are forests and deserts, below-sea-level valleys, mountains truly worthy of the term "towering," and a climate that varies from hot along the Mexican border to close to frigid in Alaska. Nestled among these many and varied habitats are a wondrous variety of fauna. One can find bison, cougars, and Douglas' squirrels; condors, ravens, and lazuli buntings; an immense diversity of invertebrates; and the reptiles and amphibians—the herpetofauna.

Among the reptiles, there are the snakes—147 species and subspecies of them, as a matter of fact. In the American west there are snakes to fill almost every ecological niche. Some are secretive woodland dwellers, some virtually "swim" beneath the surface of hot desert sands, and others inhabit cold montane streams. There is even one that has adapted to life in the ocean. You will meet them all in these pages.

The American west, as defined for the coverage of this book, is the vast region from the Pacific Ocean to the eastern borders of the states of New Mexico, Colorado, Wyoming, and Montana. We have also included the noncontiguous state of Alaska (which has only a single snake species, at its southernmost tip), and the mid-Pacific Islands of Hawaii, which, despite their tropical lushness, are home to only two snake species. One, the pelagic, ocean-going, yellow-bellied sea snake, occurs naturally in Hawaiian waters, while the second, the tiny, burrowing, introduced Asian species called the Brahminy blind snake, has been present since at least 1930. There is a possibility that a third species, the very adaptable, large, highly

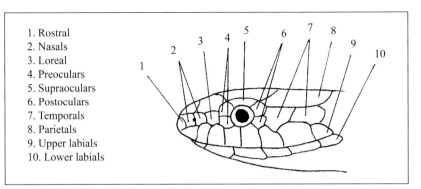

1. Rostral
2. Nasals
3. Loreal
4. Preoculars
5. Supraoculars
6. Postoculars
7. Temporals
8. Parietals
9. Upper labials
10. Lower labials

Side view of snake head

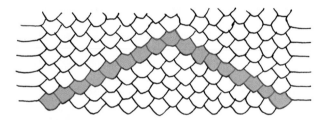

Method for counting scale rows

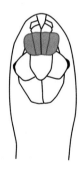

Top of snake head, showing 4 prefrontals (typical of gopher snakes and bullsnakes)

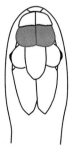

Top of snake head, showing 2 prefrontals (typical of most snakes)

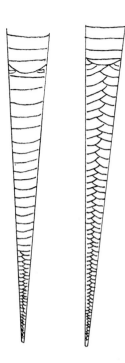 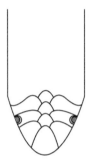

Underside of snake tail, showing entire and divided subcaudals

Head of blind snake

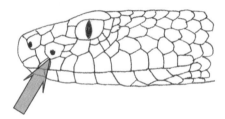

Pit viper head; arrow points to heat-sensory pit

Eastern Worm Snake   Midwest Worm Snake

Head of eastern worm snake and Midwest worm snake

predaceous, rear-fanged brown tree snake, *Boiga irregularis*, a snake that could prove to be an ecological disaster to the islands, will eventually become established.

At the opposite extreme from the small array of species of Alaska and Hawaii, we have those of the states of Arizona and California. Arizona has about 66 species and subspecies of snakes; California has a few more. There are several dangerously venomous snakes in each of these states.

How do you go about finding snakes? The finding of many species can be defined in one word—luck! (and if a second word were used it would be "perseverance")—good luck if you're *trying* to find them and do succeed, bad luck if you're *hoping* to avoid them and don't succeed.

Some species may be rather easily found basking on, or crossing, sun-warmed roadways from shortly before dusk, when temperatures begin to moderate, to well after darkness has enveloped the land. Some secretive species are surface active only after dark; even then they may be rarely encountered. You may find some snakes by turning surface rocks or discarded construction debris. Some, like the brown vine snake, are not only rare in the United States, but are so well camouflaged that unless they happen to be moving, you may look directly at one and still not be aware of its presence.

Despite their external differences, snakes and lizards (and amphisbaenians) were derived from a common ancestor. The two groups share more than seventy derived characteristics. Lizards and snakes are classed as squamates. The squamates are the most diverse living clade of recent reptiles. A clade is defined as a branch of biological taxa (species) that share features inherited from a common ancestor. Studied characteristics indicate that lizards are the older group and that snakes descended from them. Simply stated, snakes are essentially limbless lizards. Among other characteristics, squamates bear horny scales on their skin, they have movable quadrate bones, and males have hemipenes.

There is a tendency to classify snakes as harmless, mildly venomous, or dangerously venomous. These terms are actually a simplification of a complex subject. Many of the snakes called harmless, the garter and hog-nosed snakes among them, have complex saliva that may produce a startling (but usually not medically significant) reaction at the bite site. Lividity and edema figure among the symptoms. A bite from some of the smaller snake species termed mildly venomous (such as the rear-fanged black-headed and night snakes) produces fewer symptoms than a bite from some "harmless species." Because many are reluctant to bite, the significance of a bite from some of the larger rear-fanged species remains unknown. Those snakes termed dangerously venomous are just that, and include in the United States the various pit vipers, sea snakes, and coral snakes. Steer well clear of all snakes included in these three latter groups. If bitten by any, seek medical assistance as quickly as possible.

Because they are immensely interesting, snakes are often kept as captives. Be aware that many states have laws regulating the capture and/ or keeping of either or both indigenous and exotic snakes. Familiarize yourself with the laws, and be aware that if a snake is collected in violation of a state law, and then taken across a state line, the violation becomes a federal offense. Additionally, the Endangered Species Act of 1973 provides federal protection for a few snake species now considered endangered or threatened.

The keeping of venomous snakes by a hobbyist may require a permit issued by a regulatory body. We stress that no matter how knowledgeable a keeper may be, the handling or keeping of venomous snakes should be viewed as a dangerous and potentially expensive undertaking. It is estimated that in 2007 the treatment of a bite from a venomous snake cost upward of $30,000! Additionally, the negative publicity generated by an envenomation brings heightened and undeserved prejudice to bear on venomous serpents.

HOW TO USE THIS BOOK

In these pages we discuss 146 species and subspecies of snakes. While many are of very dissimilar appearance, some look confusingly alike.

To add to identification problems, some of these species have two or more color phases, which makes it difficult to categorize these creatures by color or pattern.

Therefore, we have opted to list and discuss all in a traditional manner, divided by families, subfamilies, genera, species and subspecies, and color variants, all listed alphabetically.

We have fully listed and numbered all species and subspecies in a species list following the table of contents. The numbers assigned there coincide with the numbers assigned in both text and photographs.

A COMMENT ON TAXONOMY

Despite their singularity of form, snakes are sufficiently variable structurally to allow taxonomists to group them into several different families. Further, within several of the families are groupings termed subfamilies, followed by the now-familiar genus (plural, genera), species, and subspecies.

There are some 2,400 species of snakes in the world, ranging in size from the enormity of the largest members of the family Boidae (constrictors such as the Asian reticulated python and Neotropical green anaconda, which may attain 30 feet in length) to the few inches of some of the smaller blind snakes of the family Typhlopidae.

The science of classification is called taxonomy. As in any other discipline, there are diverging beliefs, techniques, and applications.

Those of you familiar with our eastern and central guide series will note some major taxonomic changes in this western series. Familial changes are the result of an exhaustive study of genetic data by Robin Lawson and colleagues. Titled *Phylogeny of the Colubroidea (Serpentes): New Evidence from Mitochondrial and Nuclear Genes*, the completed stabilizing data are now available to all.

Because traditional systematics has "worked well" over the years, and because we feel that a field guide is not the proper forum for arguing taxonomic principles, we have continued to take a comfortable and conservative approach in these pages. Only well-accepted nomenclatural changes have been incorporated, but we include many more controversial taxonomic suggestions that have been made. There will be time for additional changes, if pertinent, later, when agreement is more general.

Wherever we felt it possible, both the common and scientific names used in this book are those suggested in the publication titled *Scientific and Standard English Names of Amphibians and Reptiles of North America North of Mexico, with Comments Regarding Confidence in Our Understanding*. This publication is the result of study and consideration by a panel of eminent herpetologists, chaired by Brian I. Crother.

ABOUT THE RANGE MAPS

When an area the size of the American and Canadian west is reduced to a range map of some 1½ × 1½ inches in size, there is little hope for precision.

This is especially true when, within a region, a particular snake may be found only in isolated patches of loose sand, along montane streams, or in other localized and specific habitats. The maps should be used only as a guide, a way to make you aware that you are somewhere close to the range of a given species or subspecies and to help you eliminate noncontending look-alikes from the list of possibilities.

ABOUT SNAKES IN GENERAL

Reptiles, as a group, arose from the amphibians, but current thoughts regarding their evolution vary widely. It is rather generally thought that the earliest reptiles appeared about 315 million years ago, in the early Upper Carboniferous period. It is from these reptiles, which were quite lizardlike in characteristics, that modern-day reptiles are thought to have evolved. As mentioned, snakes are thought to have evolved, about 135 million years ago (during the Lower Cretaceous), from lizards, and through the ensuing eons, have proven immensely successful. Snakes of some primitive families still retain vestiges of pelvic girdles (boas and pythons even retain external remnants of hind limbs, referred to as pelvic spurs) that indicate their relationship to lizards. And advanced research has divulged that monitors and beaded lizards are actually more closely allied to the snakes than to other lizards. Today, the extant snake families (which, varying by authority, may be as few as 11 or as many as 19) contain about 435 genera, and 2,400 (or more) species. Of these, there are 7 families, 35 genera, and 84 species in the American west, western Canada, and Hawaii.

Because they are ectothermic (cold-blooded), snakes utilize energy less rapidly when cool than when warm. By basking they regulate their body temperature to the level that is most beneficial to them.

All snakes are predators. Some, because of immense size, are very near the top of the food web. Others are so small and innocuous that, if seen, may be eaten by small perching birds, or even toads and frogs. Most other snake species, including those with venom, are somewhere between these two extremes. Most healthy snakes can go for a considerable time between meals without ill effects.

Some snakes actively hunt their prey, depending primarily on their acute vision (racers and whipsnakes), gliding sinuously and almost silently along through the leaves and grasses, head elevated ("periscoped"), or may trail prey by following scent trails. Other snakes are "wait and ambush" hunters, positioning themselves along rodent trails or in other strategic locations, and patiently waiting, for hours, or days, for a prey animal to pass.

Snakes subdue their prey in several ways. Constriction and envenomation are the two best-known methods. Merely grasping a prey animal and immobilizing it by throwing a loop of body over it, or simply swallowing the prey animal alive are methods also utilized.

When envenomation is employed, snakes with fixed (nonmovable) fangs usually grasp the prey and retain their grip while the venom does its work. However, the pit vipers, which have long, movable fangs and deliver the venom in a fast strike, allow their prey to run off, then follow the scent trail (the tongue carries scent particles left by the prey to the Jacobson's Organ in the palate for analysis) to the dead or dying animal and eat it (usually) after its death is ascertained. Likewise, when constriction is utilized (among others, rat snakes, gopher snakes, and kingsnakes employ this method), the prey is often not swallowed until after it is dead. Constriction does not break bones, but does tighten until inhalation is impossible. Burrowing snakes may rely on earth vibrations and scent, more than sight, to locate prey. Indeed, some snakes (blind snakes) rely on their eyes so little that these organs, so important to most, have become nonfunctional. Some snakes have developed labial (lip) pits (boas and pythons) or loreal pits (pits on the side of the face between, but lower than, the eye and nostril [rattlesnakes]) that are sensitive to minute temperature changes, such as those produced by the approach of an endothermic (warm-blooded) animal.

Snakes swallow their prey whole. Because a snake's skin is capable of considerable stretching and the jawbones are connected to the skull with muscles and ligaments rather than bone, and because the lower jaw consists of two unconnected bones, snakes can swallow comparatively immense prey. The snake usually swallows the prey nose first, moving first one side of both jaws forward, easing the prey slowly down the throat, then repeating the process with the other side, and doing this again and again. Once the prey is in the throat, the swallowing process is assisted by muscular contractions and body curves anterior to the prey that slowly force the prey into the stomach.

The scales covering snakes are merely intricate folds of skin. The finished product may be smooth and shiny, or dull and bear a keel, or roughened and rasplike, like the scales of a sea snake, or lengthened and with a free edge, like the belly scales of most snakes. The scales may be of one or more than one color, and the interstitial skin (the skin between the scales) may be colored similarly or differently. When a snake's body is distended, such as with a meal or when a female is heavily gravid, the interstitial skin may be visible, adding hues not normally seen. A snake sheds its skin at strategic times during its life. The causative agents are many and complex. Shedding is associated with growth, with the replenishment of the moisture-impervious lipid barrier, and with pheromone dispersal, but occurs at some rather well-defined times in the life of a snake. Among these are following emergence from dormancy, prior to parturition, or following the healing of an injury. Young, fast-growing snakes shed more frequently than old adults. For a few days prior to shedding, colors and patterns are dulled and a bluish cast is noticeable. The eyes become so clouded that vision is impaired. When the newly formed skin is suitably developed, the eyes clear, the old epidermis is nudged free of the lips, and as the snake crawls forward, pushing against irregularities, rocks, and vegetation, it inverts and crawls free of the old skin. Everything, including the transparent brille (eye plate), is shed. This process is referred to as ecdysis.

Snakes may move sinuously, pressing the outer edges of body curves against substrate irregularities, or may move straight ahead while paired muscles move their belly scales forward, then rearward, in rhythmic waves. The sharpened trailing edge of each belly scale (if applicable) moves the snake forward by pressing against substrate irregularities. Heavy-bodied snakes such as rattlesnakes often employ this method of slow forward movement when not frightened. Sidewinders, of course, are notorious for their looping method of progression, which moves them in a direction different from that in which the head is directed. Snakes may climb in one or more of three ways. They may simply proceed upward through a thicket by draping their body over various branches. Some snakes may climb a trunk by grasping it with a partial looping of the anterior body, then drawing the rear of the body upward, anchoring it, and pushing the anterior upward again. Other snakes, like the rat snakes, have belly scales that are angled sharply upward at their outer edges, forming corners that can catch nearly any irregularity in a tree's bark. These snakes can progress nearly straight up a trunk.

By using a side-to-side sculling motion, most snakes can swim well. However, some are surface swimmers that have difficulty submerging, while others swim easily well below the surface and may seek prey such as fish, frogs, or invertebrates while underwater. Having a flattened paddle-like tail, the sea snakes are aquatic specialists, swimming well when necessary or drifting placidly when at rest.

Snakes are ectothermic. That is, their body temperature is controlled by external conditions. To survive, snakes must keep their body temperature within suitable temperature parameters. To accomplish this most efficiently, snakes seek suitable microclimates. When their body temperature is suboptimal, snakes are affected adversely. The same holds true if they overheat. The process of controlling body temperature is called thermoregulation. Where and when climatic conditions are so adverse that thermoregulation and, hence, bodily functions become impossible, snakes brumate (the reptilian equivalent of hibernation). This period of dormancy may last for several days, several weeks, or several months. It may be instigated by the cold, by excessive heat, or even by drought. Not all snakes have the same thermal tolerances, but they all know where areas of safe haven are located within their home ranges. To successfully overwinter, a snake must have adequate fat reserves and be well hydrated when entering brumation. While active, snakes thermoregulate by seeking shade on hot days, basking in patches of sunlight on cold days, or altering their activity periods from day to night or vice versa.

Some snakes lay eggs (oviparity), some retain the eggs and birth live young while having no amniotic connection with the mother (ovoviviparity), while others are truly viviparous. Not all females breed annually. Some species, and especially viviparous species in cold climes, may breed only every second, third, or even fourth year. Males may indulge in ritualized fights to establish breeding rights and territorial dominance.

Reproductively receptive females emit pheromones that allow males to trail them, sometimes over long distances. Breeding may involve a male holding a female immobile with loops of his body and/or by biting her on the nape. Prior to breeding, some stylized courtship may occur. This may vary from cloacal region stimulation of the female by the spurs of the males, to body vibrations, to rubbing of the female's nape by the male's chin. Actual breeding may occur while the male and female snakes have their tails entwined or when the tail of the male is positioned beneath or beside that of the female. If the female finds her suitor suitable, she will lift her tail and open her cloaca, allowing the intromission by one of the male's two hemipenes. Copulation may last from minutes to hours, depending on the circumstances and species involved. To successfully breed, a snake must have adequate fat reserves. This is especially so with females.

A month or so following a successful breeding, a female of an oviparous species will lay a clutch of eggs in a protected, moisture-retaining area. Some females may produce a second clutch a month or so later. The eggs take two weeks (smooth green snakes) to 100 days to hatch. The incubation duration for most species is between 55 and 70 days. It may take the females of live-bearing species three or four months following breeding to produce their clutch. Live-bearing species seldom produce multiple clutches in a single season.

SNAKE CARE

Captive care information in a field guide?

Although we do not advocate collecting any wildlife from the wild for commercial purposes, we do strongly believe that any person interested in keeping a nonrestricted reptile or amphibian should be able to do so. Having accurate husbandry information immediately available may ease the transition for the snake. Not all snakes from the American west are equally easy to keep, nor are all of equal interest to most observers. (Most interest has always been shown in the nonregulated, constricting lampropeltines, then to a lesser degree in garter snakes, hog-noses, and lastly the venomous species). To keep venomous or restricted species you may need a local, state, or federal permit.

We do not delve deeply into captive care, but have included the basics, such as preferred foods and reproductive biology, in each family account. A great many books are available that provide detailed husbandry information, but the basics are pretty standard:

1. Dry, clean, *escape-proof* caging *of suitable size* will be needed. Snakes are escape artists par excellence. Choose the caging wisely. In most cases, an aquarium will suffice nicely, and clip-on tops are readily available at pet stores.
2. Suitable substrate is needed. This may be clean newspapers, unbleached paper towels, aspen shavings, or, for burrowing species, clean sand of the type in which they were found. We suggest against using sharp-grained silica play sand available at home

improvement stores. If the substrate is allowed to become fouled or too wet (or especially fouled *and* too wet), the snakes in that cage will often develop unsightly, difficult to cure, and sometimes lethal skin lesions.

3. Suitable cage temperature; somewhat variable by species, but try to provide a thermal gradient. A daytime temperature of 86–100°F on the hot end of the cage, and not lower than 70°F on the cool end, is usually fine for desert species. Montane forms will prefer their cage a bit—maybe 5°—cooler.

4. A water container, always with fresh water. The relative size of this may vary by species. A sand-dune–dwelling species can be kept with only a small container of water, while a species that immerses itself to soak periodically will need a greater amount of water. Since snakes are ectothermic (cold-blooded) creatures, the ability to remain in prime health is directly related to the continuous availability of fresh water in their cage and to the cage temperature.

5. A hide box should be provided. Snakes thrive best when they feel secure.

6. Suitable food—both in type and in quantity—should be readily available. We urge you to feed your snake prekilled prey.

If you can't get your snake to feed within a reasonable period of time (from four to six weeks), it should be released exactly where it was found (keep in mind that captive-bred snakes should *never* be released). The appetite of many snakes will diminish (or they may cease to feed entirely) in the winter, even if warm cage temperatures are maintained. This is normal behavior.

In addition to books, at least three other excellent sources of husbandry information exist. These are herp expos, herpetological societies, and the Internet. Herp expos are many-vendor sales of reptiles, amphibians, and support equipment. Expos are held periodically in many of the larger cities in the United States, Canada, and Europe. Herpetological societies can be found in many of the larger cities. Information on herp societies can be obtained from pet stores, museums, or similar sources. Myriad Web sites provide interactive chat rooms, forums, and information on both common and rare species.

Hypomelanistic California Kingsnake

Most captive snakes are easily cared for and housed. This is especially true of the rat snakes and kingsnakes, the water snakes, the garter snakes, and the hog-nosed snakes. Several of the tiny burrowing species will require specialized insect diets.

The rodent- and bird-eating snakes seem to get enough calcium in their diets and so do not seem to need full-spectrum lighting in order to maintain calcium levels in their blood. These snakes require feeding only once a week and some need it even less often.

Insect-eating snakes fed crickets may need vitamin D3-calcium supplements. They should be provided with food every two or three days except when they are in their shedding cycle.

When planning a caging setup, do not be deceived by a snake's name. For example, although they are called water snakes, the semiaquatic species in the genus *Nerodia* need areas where they can emerge from the water and fully dry off. They will quickly develop potentially fatal skin lesions if they are kept perpetually wet.

Today, commercial reptile cages of many shapes and sizes are available. It is no longer necessary to convert aquaria into terraria, although it is certainly perfectly acceptable to do so. No matter the source of your caging, be certain that the terrarium/cage is tightly covered.

Provide your snake with cage furniture; climbing limbs, an easily cleaned substrate, and a hiding box are a good start. The very slender and almost feather-light brown vine snake is at home in twig-tip foliage, but even it prefers the stability offered by vine tangles. Perches or limbs should be a minimum of one and a half times the diameter of the snake's body.

By nature, snakes are secretive beasts, but some hide more persistently than others, especially during the daylight hours. Snakes always do best as captives when they feel safe and secure. Although perfectly hardy, the various milk snakes are among the most secretive of snakes. These creatures will probably spend most of their time beneath the substrate. The larger kingsnakes do much the same. Gopher snakes, rat snakes, garter snakes, and ribbon snakes will prefer a hidebox that is barely big enough for them to coil within.

Provide your snake the ability to thermoregulate in its cage. This may be accomplished with an undertank heater under one part of the cage or with an overhead light over one end. Because hot rocks have malfunctioned and burned the snake(s) using them, we do not recommend them.

If your snake is "opaque" or "blue," the condition assumed prior to skin-shedding when the snake's eyes actually take on a blue or cloudy coloration, add a water dish, large enough to allow your snake to soak, in the cage. This can be replaced with a smaller drinking dish once the snake has actually shed.

Naturally changing weather patterns—dry seasons, rainy seasons, low-pressure frontal systems, the high pressure associated with fine weather, even the lunar cycle—are known to affect snake behavior. Many nocturnal snakes are most active during the dark of the moon or during unsettled weather. Reproductive behavior is often stimulated by the elevated humidity and lowering barometric pressures that occur at the advent of a storm.

Despite being carnivorous, snakes exhibit many degrees of dietary specialization. Some undergo age-related changes in diet preferences. Rat snakes are among these. In the wild, the hatchlings of many rat snakes eat lizards and frogs (especially treefrogs), but with increasing age become efficient and preferential predators of rodents (and birds). For a captive snake to eat properly, you must offer it the correct type of food in a setting the snake finds secure.

There are two things that you can do if your snake is a temperate species and a winter nonfeeder. You can cool the animal into a state of dormancy (this is most natural for the snake), or you can fuss with it, changing lighting, warmth, and feeding parameters, and hope that you hit on the combination that induces the snake to feed. In most cases, the cooling is the easier of the two. If your snake is one of those that stops eating seasonally, it is imperative that it be at optimum weight (a little on the heavy side of normal) as autumn approaches.

A growing body of evidence suggests that what is a natural diet for a snake is the best diet in captivity. Although in the wild many snakes eat a diet consisting of primarily one type of prey (rat snakes and rodents), others are entirely opportunistic in their feeding preferences (kingsnakes). Humans have a tendency to feed all snakes the prey items most easily obtained. Thus, we strive to adapt hog-nosed snakes (snakes that normally feed upon toads and frogs as well as occasional rodents) to a diet of mice, and we try our best to get the salamander- and snake-eating ring-necks on a diet of pink mice. On such a contrived diet these snakes may not only refuse to breed but have a lessened lifespan as well.

KEY TO THE FAMILIES OF NORTH AMERICAN SNAKES

1a. Tail flattened, paddle-like, marine environments . . . .**Pelamidae, Sea Snake**

1b. Tail basically cylindrical 2

2a. Tail tipped with segmented horny rattle 3

2b. Tail with no terminal rattle 4

3a. Crown scales very small (fragmented). Loreal pit always present. Movable fangs at front of upper jaw. **Venomous** . . . .**Viperidae, Rattlesnakes** (in part)

3b. As above but crown scales large and platelike (unfragmented). **Venomous** . . . . **Viperidae, Pygmy Rattlesnakes and Massasaugas**

4a. No enlarged scales on belly. 5

4b. Enlarged scales on belly. 6

5a. Size, tiny. No functional external eyes. Smooth, shiny scales. Tail blunt, tipped with spine. Teeth only in lower jaw. 14 scale rows . . . . **Leptotyphlopidae, Slender Blind Snakes**

5b. As in 5a, but teeth only in upper jaw. 16 scale rows. . . . . **Typhlopidae, Typical Blind Snakes**

6a. Body scales small. Tail short and tapering or short and bluntly rounded. Crown scales fragmented or entire. Pupils elliptical. Ventral (belly) scutes enlarged but proportionately narrow. Labial pits present but variably discernable. Loreal pit never present. No movable fangs at front of upper jaw .... **Boidae, Rosy and Rubber Boas**

6b. Not as in 6a 7

7a. Crown (top of head) plates not fragmented. Tail tapering. Color and pattern variable (including black, red, and yellow or white saddles, bands, or rings; if of these colors, the caution colors of red and yellow are usually separated by black, or there is flecking of white in the black and of black in the red.) No fangs in the front of the upper jaw . . . .**Colubridae** (in part), **"Harmless" Snakes**

7b. Patterned in broad rings (not bands or saddles) of black, red, and yellow or white (caution colors of red and yellow touching). Very short fixed fangs at front of upper jaw. Note: Rarely, one of the three colors may be reduced or absent. **Venomous. . . . . Elapidae, Coral Snakes**

2

Slender Blind Snakes, Family Leptotyphlopidae

Within this family are nearly eighty species contained in two genera. Of these, only three species in a single genus, *Leptotyphlops*, occur in the United States. Both species occur west of the Mississippi River. The blind snakes in this family have teeth only in their lower jaw and have the untoothed maxillary bones fused solidly to the skull. Facial and crown scalation will help differentiate the species. A hand lens may be necessary to see scale details of these tiny snakes. None have toxin.

Slender blind snakes lack enlarged ventral scutes and functional eyes. They are persistent burrowers that surface occasionally in the spring and autumn and when summer rains flood their burrows. They are often seen on aridland roadways on humid or wet nights. These snakes feed largely on the larvae and pupae of ants, but subterranean termites and the burrowing larvae of some beetles are also accepted. The snakes in this family are oviparous. Clutch size is from one to six (rarely more) eggs. Eggs, and gravid females, have been found in July as much as 2½ feet underground in communal chambers.

When handled, frightened, or attacked by ants, these snakes may tip the body scales slightly forward. They then appear silvery in color. If grasped, these snakes often press the tailtip spine against the hand of its captor, a startling, but harmless ploy.

Taxonomic note: Many authorities refer to the snakes in this genus as thread snakes.

1. New Mexican Blind Snake

Leptotyphlops dissectus

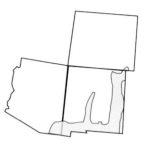

Abundance/Range: This is a common to abundant species in suitable habitats. At times, more than a half dozen individuals may be found under a single piece of suitable debris. This snake occurs both to the north and the south of the international boundary from southeastern Arizona, eastward to Val Verde County in west Texas, then northward to southwestern Kansas and extreme southeastern Colorado. A probably disjunct population exists in central Mew Mexico.

Habitat: This snake burrows persistently, thus is seldom seen. It may be surface active in the evening in warm weather, or during or after heavy rains. It occurs in sandy, yielding soils, where it is most frequently found beneath moisture retaining natural and human-generated ground-surface debris.

New Mexican Blind Snake

Size: When adult this blind snake is rarely more than 9½ inches long (10¾ inches is the record size). Most specimens found are between 5 and 8 inches in length. Hatchlings are about 2¾ inches in length.

Identifying features: Although lacking annulations, this little snake looks superficially like an earthworm. It is a shiny, but pale, brown to pinkish brown dorsally, and paler below. This snake has a blunt nose and a spine-tipped, blunt tail. There are no enlarged belly plates, and the head, neck, and body are all the same diameter. The eyes are present, but buried beneath a translucent scale and basically nonfunctional. There are three crown scales and two supralabial scales. The jaw is countersunk, and the anal plate is not divided.

Similar snakes: The subspecies of the western blind snake, *Leptotyphlops humilis* have only one crown scale.

Comments: Until recently, the New Mexican blind snake was considered a subspecies of the plains blind snake, *L. dulcis*.

2. Southwestern Blind Snake

Leptotyphlops humilis humilis

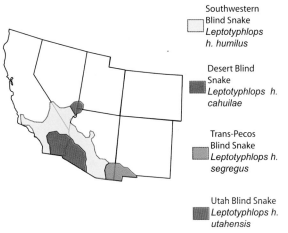

Southwestern Blind Snake
Leptotyphlops h. humilus

Desert Blind Snake
Leptotyphlops h. cahuilae

Trans-Pecos Blind Snake
Leptotyphlops h. segregus

Utah Blind Snake
Leptotyphlops h. utahensis

Abundance/Range: This common but seldom seen snake ranges widely over much of southern and central Arizona, northward to the southernmost tip of Nevada, westward to the coast of southern California, and southward along the Pacific coast of Baja to mid-peninsula.

Habitat: Although an arid-land form, like other blind snakes, it does need some soil moisture. It is most often found beneath moisture-retaining surface debris, but is fully capable of digging deeply in its search for moist environs.

Size: Adult at 6–12 inches, this snake occasionally attains 14 inches in length.

Southwestern Blind Snake

Identifying features: A single interocular scale is present. The eyes are visible as dark spots beneath the translucent ocular plates. The head, neck, and body are of similar girth. The lower jaw is noticeably countersunk. Both head and tail are blunt; the tail is tipped with a tiny spine. The belly plates are not enlarged. There are 12 rows of scales ringing the tail. This race has 7–9 strongly pigmented (purplish) rows of dorsal scales.

Similar species: *Leptotyphlops dissectus* has 3 scales between the ocular scales; see account 1. The silvery legless lizard has eyelids.

Comments: The four subspecies are collectively referred to as "western blind snakes." The various subspecies are not recognized by many researchers.

ADDITIONAL SUBSPECIES

The characteristics that differentiate the subspecies are relatively minuscule, and can be difficult to ascertain. Rely principally on range for identification purposes.

3. The Desert Blind Snake, *L. h. cahuilae,* occurs in southeastern California and southwestern Arizona. With a record length of 15½ inches, this is the largest of the western blind snakes. There are 12 rows of scales ringing the tail and 5 weakly pigmented (purplish) dorsal scale rows.

Desert Blind Snake

4. The Trans-Pecos Blind Snake, *L. h. segregus,* is the easternmost representative of this species. It ranges westward along the Rio Grande, from Val Verde County, Texas, to Santa Cruz County, Arizona. This race has only 10 rows of scales ringing the tail.

Trans-Pecos Blind Snake

5. The Utah Blind Snake, *L. h. utahensis,* may be found in southwestern Utah and adjacent Arizona and Nevada. This race has 12 rows of scales ringing the tail and 7 purplish (pigmented) dorsal scale rows.

Utah Blind Snake. Photo by Brian Eager

3

Blind Snakes, Family Typhlopidae

The three genera in this primarily tropical family contain more than 160 species. All are persistent burrowers. None are native to the United States, but one, the Brahminy blind snake, has been introduced to the southern half of peninsular Florida, has now been found in the Lower Rio Grande Valley of Texas and more recently in southern coastal California, and is firmly established on most of the islands in the Hawaiian chain. In this family the maxillary bones are toothed and are *not* fused solidly to the skull. The lower jawbones bear no teeth. The Brahminy blind snake is a unisexual, parthenogenetic, oviparous, all-female species. Gravid blind snakes have been found throughout most warm months of the year, and may breed year-round. Between 2 and 8 (usually 2–4) eggs are produced in each clutch.

6. Brahminy Blind Snake

Ramphotyphlops braminus

Abundance/Range: This very common snake occurs on most of the principal Hawaiian Islands. It also occurs in Australia, Asia, Latin America, and elsewhere in tropical and subtropical regions of the world.

Habitat: This snake prefers areas of loose, warm soil that retain at least vestiges of moisture. It can be abundant in irrigated areas such as lawns and gardens, and is often found in the soil of potted plants and beneath surface debris.

Size: This tiny snake is adult at about 5 inches in length. Specimens up to 6½ inches have been found. Hatchlings are about 2½ inches long.

Brahminy Blind Snake

Identifying features: This little snake has 14–20 rows of smooth, shiny, dark gray to black scales. Impending ecdysis (skin shedding) renders the snake silvery blue in appearance. The belly is lighter. The chin, throat, anal region, and underside of the tip of the tail are often particularly pale. The ventral scales are not enlarged. Both head and tail are blunt. There is a tiny tailtip spine. The eyes are rudimentary and covered by a large, translucent scale. The lower jaw is countersunk. The scales ring this snake's body in 18–20 rows at midbody. There is no enlarged anal plate.
Similar Snakes: None in Hawaii.

4

Boas, Family Boidae

Rosy and Rubber Boas, Subfamily Ericinae

Boas are primitive snakes. The two genera in the western United States are of stocky build and small size. All boas are nonvenomous, powerful constrictors. Vestiges of the pelvic girdle remain. A tiny movable spur is present on each side of the vent. The spurs, remnants of hind limbs, are most prominent on males; those of the females may actually be hidden in a pocket of skin. The spurs are used by males during courtship. A coronoid bone is present in the lower jaw. Rubber boas have large platelike scales on the top of the head, whereas the corresponding scales of the rosy boas are small and fragmented. Boas have vertical pupils and lack enlarged chin-shields. The subcaudal scales are not divided. The body scales are tiny and nonkeeled.

These live-bearing snakes feed on small rodents (especially nestling mice), an occasional shrew, nestlings of ground-dwelling birds, lizards, smaller snakes, salamanders, and anurans. The rubber boas are capable of forming more than a single constricting coil at one time. If rodents are encountered in a burrow where constriction is difficult or impossible, they may be merely pressed against the wall of the burrow to immobilize them.

Rubber boas produce 1–9 babies, while rosy boas may have up to 14.

Rubber boas, the more northerly of the two species, may be surface active at temperatures between 55 and 70°F. The more southerly rosy boas seem to prefer temperatures between 65 and 78°F. During the hot days and nights of midsummer, rubber boas may burrow deeply below the ground or into a shady, decomposing stump and aestivate. Both species may be become particularly active as passing storms or frontal systems lower barometric pressure.

Both rosy and rubber boas are largely crepuscular and nocturnal, but may be active by day during the breeding season.

Rubber boas ball tightly when frightened, often elevating their blunt tail above the level of the body. The sometimes heavy scarring on the tail of the rubber boa is often credited to the supposition that the rubber boa uses that member to fend off the bites of adult mice or shrews while it is raiding their nests for young.

Taxonomic note: Some authorities place both the rubber and the rosy boas in the genus *Charina*. This generic consolidation remains controversial. We therefore continue to assign the rubber boas to the genus *Charina* and the rosy boas to *Lichanura*.

Rosy Boas—Beautiful and Secretive

The rosy boas, all subspecies of *Lichanura trivirgata*, are variable, common, and coveted hobbyist favorites. They are found in California, Arizona, Sonora, and the Baja Peninsula. Three subspecies occur north of the Mexican border. Even within the populations, color and pattern may vary considerably. Some individuals may be virtually unicolored (or at least obscurely patterned) while others have prominent linear patterns. Some are pretty; others are *very* pretty.

And the one in front of me now on the road was definitely in the "very pretty" category.

continued

Ed Pirog and I had taken a night herping drive, as much just to get out as to see any particular herps. But it had been a good night. We had seen geckos of two species, granite night lizards, and a few interesting snakes. But as with all good things, it was now time to bring the jaunt to a close. Ed was driving and chose to take the long way back to the coast, an excellent decision, as it turned out.

We had just sped through a very substantial road cut and were nearing a mountain pass when I spotted a little white "stick" in the middle of the lane. I hollered, Ed skidded to a stop, and I was out of the Wrangler almost before it stopped moving.

As I neared it, the stick steadily became more snakelike. When I finally bent over the object, I was enchanted. The ground color was just a bit on the gray side of white, and the pattern consisted of well-defined spots of russet orange. It was the prettiest little rosy boa I had ever seen in the wild.

Both Ed and I left well satisfied with the evening's efforts.

7. Northern Rubber Boa

Charina bottae

Abundance/Range: Although it is secretive, and very easily overlooked, the northern rubber boa may be present in suitable habitat in considerable numbers. This boa does not seem to be in serious decline at any point in its extensive range. It ranges ranges northward from central California through western Oregon and Washington to extreme southwestern British Columbia, then eastward to south central and southeastern British Columbia, north central Wyoming, and central western Nevada.

Habitat: The northern rubber boa seeks refuge beneath decomposing logs and other surface debris and rocks. It can be particularly common at dump sites (especially at woodland edges), and during dry periods may seek the secure dampness

Northern Rubber Boa

beneath streamside debris. These snakes may also utilize the shelter provided by the loosened bark of dead standing and fallen trees. Burrows are
also utilized. It is found from sea level to elevations of more than 10,000
feet in coniferous forests, mountain meadows, grasslands and semiarid
habitats.

Size: Northern rubber boas are adult at 15–25 inches. The record size is 33
inches. Neonates are between 7½ and 9 inches in length.

Identifying features: Northern rubber boas are a unicolored tan, brown,
olive brown, or olive green above, and cream, yellowish, or yellowish
green below. The belly may be smudged with darker pigment. The scales
at midbody number 45 or more rows. The body skin appears loose, and
may fold into accordion-pleats when the snake coils, turns tightly, or con-
stricts. The tail is thick and blunt, and may be rather easily mistaken for
the head. Scars from rodent bites or other injuries are darker than the
ground color, and may make old specimens appear sparingly patterned.
The scars are often most prevalent posteriorly, and especially so on the
tail. The 192 (or more) ventral scutes are well developed, but proportionately narrow. The eyes are small, but fully functional. The babies are more
brilliantly colored than the adults, often orange brown to salmon. This
brilliance fades quickly with growth.

Similar species: There is no snake species in the North American west, except the southern rubber boa (account 8), that could be easily mistaken for a rubber boa.

ADDITIONAL SUBSPECIES

None.

8. Southern Rubber Boa

Charina umbratica

Abundance/Range: Considered a threatened species by the state of California, this little boa is found only in the San Jacinto and San Bernardino mountains. Despite its limited distribution, it may be quite common in suitable habitat.

Habitat: The southern rubber boa is found amid fallen timber and rock jumbles beneath which it seeks refuge. It may also utilize the shelter provided by loosened bark of standing trees as well as that of dead trees and stumps, and the burrows of small mammals. This snake occurs at elevations between 5,000 and 8,100 feet.

Southern Rubber Boa

Size: Adults are usually less than 24 inches in length and neonates average only 8¼ inches.

Identifying features: The southern rubber boa is a dwarfed species. The color of this snake throughout its life is usually pinkish orange to brownish orange. The belly is cream to light yellow. This species has 44 or fewer rows of scales at midbody and 191 or fewer ventral scutes.

Similar species: The northern rubber boa is larger and usually darker in coloration when adult, and has 45 or more rows of scales at midbody.

Comments: Until recently this snake was considered a subspecies of the northern rubber boa. Breeding adults may be only 11–15 inches in length.

ADDITIONAL SUBSPECIES

None.

9. Mexican Rosy Boa

Lichanura trivirgata trivirgata

Abundance/Range: This rosy boa is rather uncommon in the United States but is quite common in northwestern Mexico. It has a very limited range in the United States, where it occurs only in extreme south central Arizona, westward to the Colorado River. Much of its range is in Organ Pipe Cactus National Monument and Cabeza Prieta National Wildlife Refuge. It persists even in suburban settings, and can be common on ranchlands where rodents abound.

◼ Coastal Rosy Boa
Lichanura trivirgata roseofusca

◻ Desert Rosy Boa
Lichanura trivirgata gracia

◻ Mexican Rosy Boa
Lichanura t. trivirgata

Habitat: This boa is associated with arid and semiarid scrublands, hillsides, rocky deserts, desert oases, canyons, talus, and other such rock-strewn regions. Rosy boas often occur near canyon and desertland streams, but they are by no means restricted to such locales. These snakes are capable of burrowing but often merely seek cover beneath surface debris, amidst rocks, or in the middens of burrowing rodents.

Mexican Rosy Boa

Size: This is the smallest of the three subspecies found in the United States. It is unusual to find specimens more than 30 inches in length. Neonates are 10–12 inches in length.

Identifying features: The Mexican rosy boa has a very light (cream to straw yellow) ground color, and very precisely edged chocolate to black stripes. Neither color is infiltrated by the other. The body is stout, yet supple. A row of subocular scales separate the upper labial scales from the eye. The belly may vary from cream to the palest gray. Each ventral plate may be darkest anteriorly. Neonates are colored and patterned similarly to the adults.

Similar species: The combination of stockiness, suppleness, small head scales, no enlarged chin-shields, pattern, and rather short, but tapered tail is diagnostic.

ADDITIONAL SUBSPECIES

10. The Desert Rosy Boa, *L. t. gracia*, ranges from southern and southwestern California, eastward to southwestern and central Arizona. Adults may attain 36 inches in length and neonates are 10–14 inches long.

This boa has three tan, reddish brown, or brick red stripes against a ground color of tan to grayish beige. Sparse spotting of the stripe color may be present in the ground color. The stripes are usually very prominent, and either quite straight edged or have fine serrations, producing a zipperlike edge. It has been suggested that the terra-cotta to rust striped rosy boas of central Arizona are subspecifically distinct. However, they have not yet been formally described.

Desert Rosy Boa, California

Desert Rosy Boa, Arizona

11. The Coastal Rosy Boa, *L. t. roseofusca*, often has a darker ground color and is usually less precisely patterned and less contrastingly colored than the desert rosy boa. The ground color of the coastal rosy boa varies from brownish to olive gray to gray to bluish gray. The three stripes are brown, orange, or rust. The dorsal stripe is often the widest and most indefinite. The stripe color also occurs as scattered spots between the stripes. The venter is predominantly dark, but the posterior edge of each scute is lighter. This is the largest of the rosy boas, occasionally exceeding 3½ feet in length.

Occasional snakes from southern San Diego County, California and adjacent Baja California may be gray or brown, lacking most or all contrasting colors.

The coastal rosy boa is found from southwestern California to northern Baja California.

At least one additional recognized subspecies occurs on the Baja Peninsula.

Coastal Rosy Boa

5

Advanced Snakes, Family Colubridae

Racers, Sand Snakes, Rat Snakes, Ring-necked Snakes, Hog-nosed Snakes, and Relatives

As currently defined, this vast familial assemblage contains most of the snakes in western North America. In fact, contained within its several subfamilies are most of the snakes of the world.

Although most colubrids are generally referred to as harmless, a number of these snakes have toxic saliva, and some have enlarged teeth near the rear of the upper jaw. All should be handled carefully.

The subfamilies north of Mexico include the Colubrinae, now comprising the lampropeltines (kingsnakes, rat snakes, gopher snakes, and allies), as well as the racers, leaf-nosed snakes, vine snakes, and relatives. The ring-necked snakes, leaf-litter snakes, fangless night snakes, and sharp-tailed snakes are now in the subfamily Dipsadinae. The hog-nosed snakes are in the subfamily Xenodontinae. Finally, the Natricinae comprise the water snakes, garter snakes, and relatives. As a matter of information, some researchers consider all of the mentioned subfamilies to be full families.

The colubrine snakes vary widely in appearance and lifestyles. Many are short, stocky, and terrestrial. Some are glossy-scaled burrowers. Others are slender speedsters that may as readily ascend trees as seek refuge on the ground, and yet others are persistently arboreal, seldom descending to ground level. They vary in size from the 5 or so inches of the tiny black-headed snakes to the more than 8 feet of the very impressive bullsnake.

SUBFAMILY COLUBRINAE: RACERS, WHIPSNAKES, AND ALLIES

Racers, Genus *Coluber*

Taxonomic note: It has recently been suggested that the whipsnakes and coachwhips, traditionally in the genus *Masticophis*, should actually be contained in the genus *Coluber* with the racers. This proposal is still controversial; thus we have retained the two in separate genera.

Although there are many subspecies of racers in the eastern United States, only two forms occur in our west, the eastern and the western yellow-bellied racer. Because the ranges of the two are not extensively contiguous, there is a growing tendency by researchers to consider the western yellow-bellied racer a full species. We resist this concept. Racers are absent from vast areas in our southwest.

Generally thought of as terrestrial serpents, racers can and do climb readily.

Racers are noted for their alert demeanor, readiness to bite if molested, and considerable speed. Ontogenetic changes are marked.

Hardly could a scientific name be more erroneous than the specific designation *constrictor* that has been bestowed upon this species, for the racers are, most emphatically, *not* constrictors. They merely grasp their prey and swallow it alive, occasionally making a cursory attempt to immobilize a struggling prey item with a loop of their body, but they never constrict.

Although lizards and frogs seem the principal prey items of the adults, small rodents, nestling birds, and insects are also accepted. Juveniles accept locusts, crickets, cicadas, and non-noxious caterpillars, but will also eat suitably sized lizards and frogs as well as newborn mice and hatchling birds if they are encountered.

All members of this nonvenomous genus are oviparous and produce up to 25 eggs in each clutch. A female may occasionally lay two clutches in a season. Females may remain at the nest site for several days after oviposition. The eggs have a characteristic "pebbly" shell. Hatchlings are 8–11 inches in length.

The scales are smooth, arranged in 17 rows at midbody (usually dropping to 15 rows anterior to the vent); the anal plate is divided. The pupils are round.

The whipsnakes and the coachwhips, a more diverse group, are closely allied to the racers.

Racers and Relatives: Speedsters of Grassland and Desert

Failure. Not once or twice, but a half dozen times. The protected Alameda striped racer and the San Joaquin coachwhip are two snakes that I have been hoping to photograph. Over the years I've traveled to California from Florida on at least a dozen occasions, half of them specifically to find these snakes. I have failed each and every time. Not only have I not been able to photograph them, I have not even been able to see them!

The search for these two serpentine speedsters has taken me through some beautiful country. During the searches I have been lucky enough to see a vast array of lizards, frogs, salamanders, turtles, and other snake species—even other subspecies of the elusive target snakes—so the time and trips have certainly not been a lost cause.

I have been up and down the slopes of the mountain homeland of the Alameda racer, a beautiful golden striped serpent with a velvety black ground color. And I have watched the antics of burrowing owls and short-nosed leopard lizards on the Carizzo Plains as I searched for the sand-colored San Joaquin coachwhip.

continued

During the searches I have seen wonderful sunrises and spectacular sunsets, arrays of desert blooms that would set any mind reeling, desert rainstorms and montane thunderstorms of frightening intensity. I've sought the help of fellow researchers and I've traveled remote roadways alone as I searched for either active snakes or the suitable cover to which I felt they should be drawn.

I have failed, but these failures have brought other successes, and an unyielding resolve to continue trying.

The year 2007 is now drawing near. The Wrangler, newly serviced, is sitting quietly in the yard. As I write, new plans and the starting date of a new trip are being formulated. Somewhere and at some time my path will cross the path of these racers. And although crossed paths do not necessarily mean successful photos, at least I hope to be able to say I have seen them.

12. Eastern Yellow-bellied Racer

Coluber constrictor flaviventris

Abundance/Range: This common snake ranges widely from Iowa and Arkansas westward to central Montana and central New Mexico. An isolated population exists in central eastern Arizona.

Habitat: This snake may be found in a broad cross-section of habitats. Look for it in mesquite-prickly pear associations, in shrubby fields, in open woodlands and river-edge situations, and in grasslands. It is common in the vicinity of debris-strewn deserted homesteads, farms, and ranches.

Size: The eastern yellow-bellied racer is adult at 36–48 inches in length. Rarely, a specimen may attain or exceed a length of 5½ feet. The record size is 70 inches.

Eastern Yellow-bellied Racer
Coluber constrictor flaviventris

Western Yellow-bellied Racer
Coluber constrictor mormon

Eastern Yellow-bellied Racer, adult

Eastern Yellow-bellied Racer, hatchling

Identifying features: The dorsal ground coloration of this snake is bluish, blue gray, greenish, greenish gray, brownish green, or occasionally brown. The sides may be lighter than the dorsum. The interstitial skin and leading edges of the dorsal and lateral scales may be quite dark. Upper and lower labial scales are white to yellowish, and the venter is creamy to a rather bright yellow. This race usually has 7 upper labial scales.

The hatchlings have a ground color of tan to buff or gray with dark-edged, dark gray to brown dorsal saddles and dark spots on the side. These spots are best defined anteriorly and either fade noticeably or are absent posteriorly. The venter is light. There is no postorbital stripe.

Similar species: The very locally distributed smooth green snake is smaller, bright green dorsally and butter yellow to white ventrally. Gopher snakes have heavily keeled scales. Great Plains rat snakes have weakly keeled scales and a dark spearpoint atop their head. Glossy snakes are patterned dorsally and, at all stages of their life, have a postorbital stripe. Night snakes and lyre snakes have vertically elliptical pupils.

ADDITIONAL SUBSPECIES

13. The Western Yellow-bellied Racer, *C. c. mormon*, which some authorities consider to be a full species, ranges from south central British Columbia in the north to southern California in the south and extends as far east as western Montana and western Colorado.

This racer is very similar to the eastern yellow-bellied racer in appearance and habits. However, it has 8, rather than 7, upper labial scales.

In the American west the western yellow-bellied racer inhabits riparian situations, pond edges, meadows, pastures, and the like, where its amphibian prey may be found. It also occurs in vegetated and/or rocky semiarid lands, where it preys on lizards.

This westernmost representative of the species reportedly has smaller egg clutches than the eastern forms. Clutches seem most often to contain 4–8 eggs.

Western Yellow-bellied Racer

Coachwhips and Whipsnakes, Genus *Masticophis*

These slender speedsters are closely allied to the racers. The coachwhips and whipsnakes are alert serpents that often seek prey by periscoping their head above the surrounding grasses and ground plants. Their vision is, apparently, acute, and they seem to rely as much on visual as on chemical cues when pursuing prey. All manner of prey, from frogs, lizards, and smaller snakes (including those of their own kind), to small mammals and birds, are opportunistically eaten. Because of their response to visual cues, coachwhips and whipsnakes readily locate nests and feed on the nestlings of birds in shrubs and low trees.

Common names can be confusing. Despite being in the genus *Masticophis* (whipsnakes and coachwhips) the common names for *M. flagellum piceus* is Red Racer, while *M. lateralis lateralis* is called the California striped racer and *M. lateralis euryxanthus* is referred to as the Alameda striped racer.

The snakes of this genus are primarily diurnal and are often out and active on even the hottest of summer days.

Many of these snakes are of somewhat similar appearance. This is particularly true of the many races of coachwhip, *Masticophis flagellum* ssp., some of which occur in several color phases. Geographic location and scale row count can be important in arriving at a positive identification. The scale row count varies from 15 to 17. The scales are smooth, and the anal plate is divided.

While rather narrow (bluntly lance shaped), the head is deep and well defined from the slim neck. Whipsnakes are most often striped; coachwhips are plain or barred.

Although they would prefer a rapid and uneventful escape to a standoff, if cornered, coachwhips and whipsnakes vibrate their tail and assume a striking S, and some (especially the coachwhips) will bite strongly. Some may even approach an offending object (such as a human) as they strike. All are nonvenomous. Bite wounds should be cleansed and bandaged if bleeding.

Like the closely allied racers, the whipsnakes are oviparous. The 4–14 eggs have a characteristically pebbly shell. Hatchlings are often more than a foot in length.

14. Sonoran Whipsnake

Masticophis bilineatus

Abundance/Range: It is difficult to accurately assess populations of many of the wide-ranging whipsnakes—this one included. They are certainly not rare, but like a "will-o'-the-wisp," Sonoran whipsnakes are everywhere, and nowhere. They are often seen crossing country roads or mountain trails, or along canyon streams. This snake ranges westward from extreme southwestern New Mexico to central Arizona. The range extends far southward into Mexico.

Habitat: The Sonoran whipsnake is a habitat generalist. It is found in all but the most arid desert regions. Look for it by day as it basks or hunts in grasslands, thornscrub, open woodlands, rangelands, and in the proximity of mountain and desert streams.

Size: Although an average adult is between 3½ and 4¼ feet in length, individuals may occasionally reach 5½ feet. The extreme slenderness of this whipsnake causes it to look smaller.

Identifying features: This is a beautiful, if rather quietly colored snake. Dorsally, the head and tail are usually a warm brown (sometimes with an

Sonoran Whipsnake

olive overcast) but may be gray to nearly charcoal. The neck and midbody regions are grayer. The venter is yellowish and brightest beneath the tail. The chin is unspotted on snakes from the eastern portion of the range, but may be spotted on specimens from more westerly areas. A light stripe, best defined anteriorly, and narrowly bordered with darker pigment, is present on the upper half of scale row 3 and the lower half of scale row 4. A broader light stripe, involving most of scale row 1 and the lower half of scale row 2, is also present. A dark stripe, often broken, is present on the lowest one-third of scale row 1. A dark stripe borders the top of the upper labial scales and a short light stripe is usually present on the side of the nose. The scales are smooth and usually number 17 rows at midbody.

Similar species: The striped whipsnake has 15 scale rows at midbody. Garter snakes are proportionately stocky and have keeled scales.

Comments: This pretty snake may occasionally be seen on the grounds of the Arizona-Sonora Desert Museum, and along the roadways in Saguaro National Monument, Chiricahua National Monument, and other such places designed for general public access. Unless you are lucky enough to find a quietly resting specimen, however, you may see little more than a streak of gray as the snake crosses the roadway. The race once referred to as the Ajo Mountain whipsnake, *M. b. lineolatus*, is no longer recognized as distinct.

15. Sonoran Coachwhip

Masticophis flagellum cingulum

Abundance/Range: This is a commonly seen snake. This race of the coachwhip occurs in western Santa Cruz County and immediately adjacent Pima County, Arizona. From there it ranges far southward into Mexico.

Habitat: This is a snake of mesquite-prickly pear, palo verde-creosote bush, and other thornscrub associations, rangelands, and gravelly

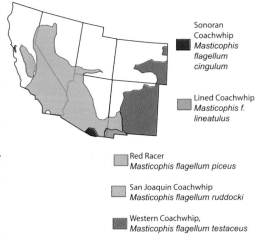

Sonoran Coachwhip *Masticophis flagellum cingulum*

Lined Coachwhip *Masticophis f. lineatulus*

Red Racer *Masticophis flagellum piceus*

San Joaquin Coachwhip *Masticophis flagellum ruddocki*

Western Coachwhip, *Masticophis flagellum testaceus*

Sonoran Coachwhip

deserts. Although it ranges far into aridlands, it is frequently encountered in riparian situations as well as around stock tanks and temporary water holes. Predominantly terrestrial, this coachwhip climbs well and regularly ascends trees and shrubs to bask and hunt.

Size: Although slender, this snake, like other races of the coachwhip, is somewhat stouter proportionately than the whipsnakes of most other species. A length of 6 feet is commonly attained.

Identifying features: The Sonoran coachwhip is typically a pinkish snake with broad, darker red to brownish red bands. The bands are usually wider than the lighter fields between them. Pattern and color are more intense anteriorly. A pale, narrow collar is usually present. The ground color may vary from pink, through tan or light reddish brown, to black. A dark longitudinal line in the center of each scale may give the appearance of keeling. Scales may also be tipped and/or edged dorsally with dark pigment, giving them a braided look.

Specimens lacking the dark bands are well known, but seem more common in Mexico than in Arizona.

The large supraocular scales partially shade the eyes and give these snakes a scowling appearance.

The large, nonkeeled scales are in 17 rows at midbody.

Similar species: See accounts numbers 16–19 for comments on additional races of the coachwhip. The Baja California coachwhip occurs in the United States only in extreme south central California. Racers of the genus *Coluber* are not red; whipsnakes (as opposed to coachwhips) are striped.

ADDITIONAL SUBSPECIES

An additional five races of coachwhip are found in the western United States. All are variable, and many can be difficult to identify with certainty. Rely on the range maps.

16. The Lined Coachwhip, *M. f. lineatulus*, seems less variable in color than the other races. It is a light grayish tan anteriorly and may retain that color, or become suffused with a light pink posteriorly. Dark dorsal neckbands are poorly defined or absent. The underside of the tail (subcaudal scales) may be a rather bright pink. Each anterior body scale bears a dark, longitudinal, central line. Together these produce a lineate pattern. This subspecies is found in the extreme southeastern section of Arizona,

Lined Coachwhip. Photo by Tom Van Devender

along the international boundary in New Mexico, and far southward into Mexico. It attains an adult size of about 6 feet.

17. The Red Racer, *M. f. piceus*, is also referred to as the red coachwhip. It ranges widely over most of Arizona, southern Nevada, and southern California. It intergrades widely with the western coachwhip in western Texas where coachwhips with confusing suites of characteristics exist. Intergrades between the red racer and the Baja California coachwhip, the San Joaquin coachwhip, the Sonoran coachwhip, and the lined coachwhip have also been documented. The red racer exists in three well-differentiated color morphs, as well as in several intermediate colors and patterns. The principal morphs are red and black, but a yellow phase also occurs.

The red phase is just that, primarily red dorsally and laterally, but with a variable amount of black present on the nape. The top of the head may be tan or red. Narrow light crossbars are usually present anteriorly. This color morph of this slender, 6-foot snake is remarkably beautiful.

The black phase is an unpatterned black anteriorly but some red pigment is usually visible on the posterior body and on the tail.

The yellow phase is similar to the red in all respects but the ground color, which is olive yellow.

Red Racer, red phase

Red Racer, black phase

18. The San Joaquin Coachwhip, *M. f. ruddocki*, now an uncommon snake, is protected by the state of California. It is thought that its scarcity is due to habitat degradation in California's San Joaquin Valley. This coachwhip has ground color of tan, grayish brown, or yellowish brown, pinkish, or reddish. It lacks a contrastingly colored head, and if neckbands are present, they are poorly defined. The belly may be lighter than the dorsum in color, and the subcaudal scales are tan to pale pink.

San Joaquin Coachwhip

San Joaquin Coachwhip

19. The Western Coachwhip, *M. f. testaceus*, is occasionally referred to as the "central coachwhip." This large snake ranges westward from central Texas and southwestern Nebraska to western New Mexico. It is immensely variable in both pattern and ground color.

The pattern variations include "unicolored" (no contrasting dark bands), narrow banded (common), and broad banded (generally less common, but predominant in some areas). The colors may be tan, olive brown, yellow brown, dark brown, silvery gray, or red of many shades. Although dark nape markings may be present, they are almost never in the form of strongly contrasting bars.

With a record size of 6 feet 8 inches, this is one of the largest races of coachwhip.

Western Coachwhip, tan phase

Western Coachwhip, red phase

20. Baja California Coachwhip

Masticophis fuliginosus

Taxonomic comment: This snake has recently been elevated from a subspecies of *Masticophis flagellum* to a full species.

Abundance/Range: Common for the full length of the Baja Peninsula, this coachwhip is uncommon in the United States, where it occurs only in extreme southern San Diego County, California.

Habitat: Chaparral, thornscrub, open sandy grasslands, and rolling hills are the preferred habitats of this coachwhip. Such habitats are becoming increasingly difficult to find in southern California.

Size: The normal adult size is 5–6 feet.

Identifying features: This snake occurs in a light and a dark phase. The light phase is common on the Baja Peninsula. It is yellowish tan to light gray with a busy dorsal pattern of thin, jagged-edged dark bars. The bars are widest and darkest on the neck (in fact, the neck may be largely black) and are prominent for the first half of the snake, then decrease in size

Baja California Coachwhip, dark phase

and contrast as they near the tail. There are usually pencil-thin horizontal lines on the anterior sides.

It is the dark phase that is found in the United States. The dark phase is variably dark. It is often black with lighter sides, thin light dorsal crossbars, light lines on the anterior side, and a largely black neck and tail. The light dorsal crossbars may be prominent or almost absent. The face and sides of the neck bear a pattern of light gray or white markings.

The belly of both phases is an unmarked creamy yellow anteriorly shading to a pinkish orange posteriorly and on the underside of the tail.

Similar species: The black phase of the red racer is of superficially similar appearance. However, its sides are dark all the way to the ventral scales.

ADDITIONAL SUBSPECIES

None.

21. California Striped Racer

Masticophis lateralis lateralis

California Striped Racer
Masticophis l. lateralis

Alameda Striped Racer
Masticophis l. euryxanthus

Abundance/Range: This snake is common over much of its range. It may be seen along both slopes of the Sierra Nevadas from north central California to central Baja Norte.

California Striped Racer

Habitat: Moisture-holding canyons, riparian situations, escarpments, rocky hillsides and their associated scrublands, open woodlands, and pond edges are home to this beautiful whipsnake.

Size: Although adult at 3–4 feet in total length, occasional specimens may attain, or slightly exceed, 5 feet.

Identifying features: The dorsal coloration of this snake is brown to black. The off-white to orange belly is brightest anteriorly. The subcaudal scales are pink. The lateral stripes are cream to yellow and only 2½ scale rows wide. This species has 17 rows of scales at midbody.

Similar species: The patterns of all other whipsnakes are "busier" and less precise than that of the California striped racer. Each scale in the light lateral stripe of the desert striped whipsnake has a dark, longitudinal, central stripe. Garter snakes have keeled scales.

ADDITIONAL SUBSPECIES

22. The Alameda Striped Racer, *M. l. euryxanthus*, is a beautiful snake with stripes more brightly colored and wider than those of other species. Anteriorly the lateral stripes and the ventral scales of this snake are orange. Both fade somewhat posteriorly, but the underside of the tail brightens to a pinkish orange or a clear pink. This subspecies has wide lateral stripes involving all of scale row 4, the upper half of scale row 3 and the lower half of scale row 5 (counting up from the ventral plates). The dorsal color varies from warm (juvenile) to dark brown, or black (adult). The

Alameda Striped Racer. Photo by Karl Heinz Switak

top of the head may be a shade lighter than the body color. This, a state threatened species, is protected by California. It occurs only in a relatively small area east of San Francisco.

23. Desert Striped Whipsnake

Masticophis taeniatus taeniatus

Abundance/Range: This is a fairly common snake. It is alert and often evades detection by indulging in a stealthy retreat. The desert striped whipsnake ranges from extreme western Texas and adjacent Mexico in the south, to south central Washington in the north.

Habitat: In the southern part of its range this snake seems most frequently associated with open woodlands in mountainous terrain. Farther north it also occurs in mountain ranges, but may also be found amid desert thornscrub, in grasslands, and in juniper-studded rangelands at lower altitudes. It is often found along river or pond edges where amphibians are common and water is readily available.

Size: This pretty snake occasionally attains 6 feet in length. Most adults, however, are between 3½ and 4½ feet long.

Desert Striped Whipsnake

Identifying features: This snake has the busiest pattern of any of the whipsnakes. It is blackish to brown or gray dorsally. The gray specimens may have a bluish or greenish overcast. There is a busy pattern of (usually) three grayish white, white, or cream stripes on each side. The uppermost light stripe is the widest. It involves all of scale row 4, the upper half of scale row 3, and the lower half of scale row 5. Each scale in scale row 4 has a dark, longitudinal, central dash, making this uppermost stripe appear divided. The scales on the side of the head have white edges or spots. A narrow black vertical marking is visible behind the eye on lighter colored specimens. The belly is yellowish and the subcaudal scales are pink or coral. This whipsnake has 15 rows of scales at midbody.

Similar species: Coachwhips lack well-defined longitudinal striping. Both the Alameda and the California whipsnakes have clear-cut stripes varying from cream to orange in color. The Sonoran whipsnake can be very similar in appearance, but its uppermost light stripe is not divided by dark streaks in the center of the scales. Garter snakes have keeled scales.

ADDITIONAL SUBSPECIES

The single additional subspecies, the central Texas whipsnake, occurs east of our area of coverage.

Patch-nosed Snakes, Genus *Salvadora*

These are speedy, largely diurnal, racer relatives of moderate size and sandy to brown or buff ground colors. The enlarged, free-edged, wrap-around rostral scale is distinctive of the genus. The middorsal area is the most richly hued, and is separated from the lighter sides by prominent dark stripes. The belly is light and may be clouded with slightly darker pigment.

Lizards are the primary prey item, but amphibians, smaller snakes, and nestling rodents are opportunistically accepted. Patch-nosed snakes have acute vision and rely on it when hunting. They also quickly take note of potential danger and are quick to flee. They are primarily terrestrial, but may pursue lizards upward into shrubs. These snakes are oviparous.

Patch-nosed snakes may be active throughout the day, even in the hottest weather.

There are three species in this genus in the western United States. All have smooth scales (occasionally weakly keeled near the vent) in 17 rows at midbody, and a divided anal plate. They can be confusingly similar in appearance, and the origin of a given specimen should be carefully considered when a positive identification is attempted. Additionally, the presence or absence of a dark lateral stripe, and the scale row on which it appears, as well as the number of small scales separating the posterior pair of chin scales, are important identification criteria.

24. Mountain Patch-nosed Snake

Salvadora grahamiae grahamiae

Abundance/Range: This widespread but seldom abundant snake ranges eastward from central Arizona to west Texas. It barely enters Mexico in the states of Sonora and Chihuahua.

Habitat: This snake is usually associated with expanses of rocky, open deserts, with arid mountainsides, mesas, and buttes, and in similar, usually remote, and often unpopulated situations.

Size: Although this snake may occasionally attain a length of 3½ feet (record 37½ inches), specimens greater than 3 feet are rare. Most found are between 18 and 28 inches in length.

Identifying features: The mountain patch-nose is a precisely marked snake that often bears only the dark dorsolateral stripes, with the thin

Mountain Patch-nosed Snake

lateral lines imprecisely delineated or lacking. The buff to yellowish mid-dorsal stripe is two scale rows wide. It is bordered on either side by a dark stripe of similar width. All stripes are even edged. The eyes are large. There are 8 upper labial scales. At most, this species has only a single small scale between the rear chin scales.

Similar snakes: Patch-noses can be difficult to differentiate and identify. See accounts 25–28 for descriptions of the other patch-nosed snakes. Unless the snake is actually in hand and the locality is known, positive identification can be difficult. Garter snakes have keeled body scales.

ADDITIONAL SUBSPECIES

The larger and very precisely patterned Texas patch-nosed snake occurs to the east of the scope of this book.

25. Desert Patch-nosed Snake

Salvadora hexalepis hexalepis

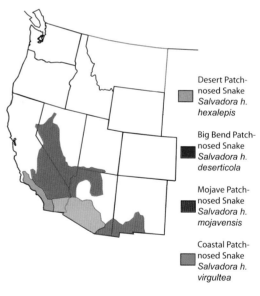

Abundance/Range: This common but well-camouflaged snake is rather easy to overlook unless your paths directly cross. This is the southeasternmost representative of the four races. It ranges westward from southeastern Arizona to south central California, and then south to eastern central Baja and central Sonora.

Desert Patch-nosed Snake *Salvadora h. hexalepis*

Big Bend Patch-nosed Snake *Salvadora h. deserticola*

Mojave Patch-nosed Snake *Salvadora h. mojavensis*

Coastal Patch-nosed Snake *Salvadora h. virgultea*

Habitat: The desert patch-nosed snake is a denizen of the arid and semiarid southwest. It occurs in brushlands, thornscrub, cactus-creosote bush associations, rocky hillsides, canyons, and other such varied areas. It often hides beneath human-generated debris and natural cover.

Desert Patch-nosed Snake

Size: While adult at 26–36 inches in length, the desert patch-nosed snake has been documented at 46 inches.

Identifying features: The upper sides and the top of the head are medium to pale gray. The middorsal stripe, 3 scale rows wide, and the lower sides are a distinct but pale yellow. The belly is cream, often shading to the palest of oranges posteriorly, especially beneath the tail. The eyes are large, and the rostral scale is very large, has free edges, and wraps up over the tip of the snout. The internasal scales are not separated by the wraparound rostral. There are 9 upper labial scales, one of which reaches the eye. The loreal scale is often divided into 2 or 4 smaller segments. The scales are in 17 rows. The scales are smooth except near the vent, where they are weakly (females), to moderately (males) keeled. The anal plate is divided.

Similar snakes: Leaf-nosed snakes are much smaller, and are blotched or spotted, rather than striped. The dark dorsolateral stripes of the mountain patch-nosed snake are usually not divided by thin, light-colored stripes.

ADDITIONAL SUBSPECIES

26. The Big Bend Patch-nosed Snake, *S. h. deserticola*, is considered a full species by some researchers. This pallid snake looks as though it has been colored in pastels. There is a broad pale middorsal stripe (about 3 scale rows wide). This is edged ventrally by a dark stripe, 2 scale rows wide.

Big Bend Patch-nosed Snake

The dark stripe is even-edged dorsally, but saw-toothed ventrally. Below the dark stripe is another light line, this one about 1½ scale rows wide. A thin, dark, lateral stripe is present 4 scales above the ventral plates. The venter is pinkish to pinkish orange. The chin is light. There are 2–7 small scales separating the posterior chin shields, and 9 supralabial scales. Two supralabial scales (usually) touch the eye. The (patchlike) rostral scale is large, free edged, curves up over the nose, and has a small groove on the ventral surface. The smooth dorsal scales are in 17 rows at midbody; the anal plate is divided. This snake ranges westward in the United States from Texas' Big Bend region to southeastern Arizona. It may also be found well southward into Mexico.

27. The Mojave Patch-nosed Snake, *S. h. mojavensis*, is a pale version of the desert patch-nosed snake that ranges from northwestern Nevada and south central Utah, southward to southern California and central Arizona. The stripes, although dark bordered and straw to pale yellow, are often not strongly in contrast with the ground color. The top of the head is brown(ish). This snake may have anterior crossbars that largely obscure the anterior striping. The loreal scale is usually not divided. The upper labials are usually separated from the eye by a few small subocular scales.

Mojave Patch-nosed Snake

28. The Coastal Patch-nosed Snake, *S. h. virgultea*, is a dark and precisely patterned snake. It ranges along the coastal strand of southern California and northern Baja Norte. It tends to have sides of light gray or sandy brown. The yellow on the lower sides is normally only 1 or 2 scale rows

Coastal Patch-nosed Snake

wide. The top of its head is usually brown. The vertebral stripe is usually only 2 scale rows wide, one full row and a half row on each side. One upper labial scale usually reaches the eye. The loreal scale is fragmented into 2 or 4 small scales.

Smooth Green Snake, Genus *Opheodrys*

The Smooth Green Snake, a tiny, secretive insectivore, is the sole representative of this bitypic genus in the American west. It is the brightest green snake in the west, and it has a yellow-tinged white belly. It appears to use visual cues when foraging, and its eyesight seems acute.

This is an oviparous species, and its clutch can contain up to 12 eggs. The usual count is between 4 and 8. Its eggs have been known to hatch in as few as 4 days but usually take 15–20 days. Hatchlings are about 5½ inches long.

The scales are smooth and in 15 rows. The anal plate is divided.

Taxonomic note: It has been suggested by some researchers that the smooth green snake should be removed from the genus *Opheodrys* and placed in the genus *Liochlorophis*.

This snake is distantly related to the racers.

29. Smooth Green Snake

Opheodrys vernalis

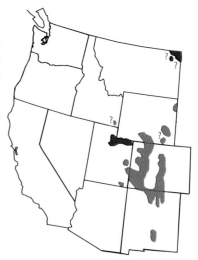

Abundance/Range: This snake remains common in some parts of its range, but has become uncommon in or absent from others. Like those of other insectivorous snakes, populations of the smooth green snake seem to have suffered adversely in areas where insecticides are regularly or heavily applied. The smooth green snake is widespread in eastern North America, but of spotty distribution in the west. West of the 100th meridian, the smooth green snake occurs in east-

Smooth Green Snake

ern Montana, Wyoming, Colorado, Utah, New Mexico, and Chihuahua, Mexico.

Habitat: This is a well-camouflaged, diurnal snake of fields and fence-rows, orchards, and meadows. It is also found in open, damp woodlands as well as shrubby clearings and woodland edges. This snake prefers moist areas, where it prowls slowly, usually in a terrestrial search for its prey. It often seeks refuge beneath logs, boards, newspaper, or other surface debris. Although the smooth green snake is fully capable of climbing, it is less prone to do so than the more southerly rough green snake. However, it often ascends into tufts of leaning grasses, low shrubs, and vines.

Size: Most smooth green snakes are between 12 and 15 inches long. Occasional specimens may near, or slightly exceed, 2 feet in length.

Identifying features: This is the only uniformly leaf green (rarely, olive) snake in the western United States. Its belly varies from white to yellow. Upper labial scales are yellow. Just before it sheds, and soon after death, its colors are muted, often gray or bluish gray. Until their postnatal shed, hatchlings are gray to olive rather than the leaf green color of the adults. Rarely, if extremely frightened, this species may gape, displaying the dark interior of its mouth.

Similar snakes: None within the scope of this book.

Vine Snakes, Genus *Oxybelis*

This genus is of Neotropical distribution. Only a single species, the brown vine snake, reaches northward into the United States, and it occurs only in the mountain canyons of extreme southeastern Arizona. Several other Neotropical species are in this genus. All are clad in hues of brown, gray, green, or combinations of those colors, and all are very well camouflaged, very slender, and primarily arboreal.

All these snakes are dubbed "mildly venomous." Little research has been done on the drop for drop toxicity. The vine snakes have well-developed, grooved fangs in the rear of their upper jaw that effectively allow venom to enter a bite wound. The toxin of all causes at least some localized to moderately generalized discomfort. Although most are reluctant to bite humans, we feel that these snakes should be treated with a great deal of care and respect.

An alert snake with keen vision, this snake always holds its head almost level, or with the nose tilted just slightly upward. It may glide swiftly away from perceived danger or move haltingly, head and neck waving slowly, looking for all the world like a broken twig swaying in the breeze. The tongue is often extended straight forward, forked tips tightly together, and held in that manner for some seconds. When threatened, this snake often gapes widely, exposing the dusky interior of its mouth, and faces the enemy, but even if lifted at this time it will seldom bite.

Little is known about the reproductive biology of this snake. One female laid 4 elongate eggs. The single hatchling that emerged was 12⅜ inches long.

30. Brown Vine Snake

Oxybelis aeneus

Abundance/Range: To attempt to approximate the population statistics of a snake as cryptic as this species is an exercise in futility. This is especially true on the periphery of a range, and in a relatively remote area. Certainly the brown vine snake is abundant just a short distance south of  the Arizona border in Mexico. However, only a few dozen specimens have been found in various canyons in its Arizona stronghold. This snake

Brown Vine Snake

ranges northward from southeastern Brazil to southeastern Arizona. In Arizona, it is known only from the Pajarito, Patagonia, and Tumacacori mountains.

Habitat: In the United States, the brown vine snake seems restricted to several semiarid canyons and their environs at elevations of 2,500–4,500 feet. The snake is persistently arboreal, but when arboreal pathways such as intertwining limbs or tree-to-tree vines are not present, it will readily descend to the ground to move from copse to copse.

Size: Most individuals of this pencil-thin snake are between 30 and 50 inches in total length. Occasional adults (especially those from Latin America) are a full 60 inches long. The excessive slenderness causes estimates of the length of most specimens to be less than they actually are.

Identifying features: This attenuate, sharp-nosed snake is unmistakable. Dorsally it is primarily a brownish (dead vine) gray, with the head and anterior neck more richly colored than the body. A darker horizontal eye stripe begins at the nostril and continues well onto the neck. The chin and ventral half of the neck are a bright yellow, fading to grayish brown on the posterior neck and continuing to the tailtip. The outer edges of the ventral scutes may bear dark flecks. The head is long, the snout sharply pointed when viewed both from above or in profile.

The nonkeeled scales are in 17 rows; the anal plate is divided; the tail is long (about two-fifths the total length) and very slender. If threatened or restrained this species will gape, displaying the dark interior of its mouth.

Similar snakes: There are no other snakes similar to the brown vine snake in the United States.

Leaf-nosed Snakes, Genus *Phyllorhynchus*

This genus of small burrowing snakes is represented in the American southwest by two species. They often emerge from their burrows after nightfall or following rains. They may then be seen crawling on the desert sands or crossing desert roadways.

Both species have a huge, free-edged, wraparound rostral scale that may help them burrow more efficiently or root out secluded prey. The oft-stated supposition that these snakes eat lizards and lizard eggs has not been borne out by captives. In fact, both species of leaf-noses have proven almost impossible to keep successfully in captivity.

Little is known with certainty about the reproductive biology of the leaf-nosed snakes. It is thought that only a single clutch containing 2–6 eggs is laid in the late spring or early summer. A single hatchling (still with egg-tooth) found crossing a roadway in late August measured very slightly more than 6 inches.

These are feisty little snakes that, if threatened, will not hesitate to draw their neck into an S and strike repeatedly. Because of their tiny size, they are not considered a serious threat.

The dorsal scales of both species are in 19 rows. The dorsal scales of the males of some subspecies are weakly keeled, while those of the females of all races are smooth. The nose is blunt. The internasal scales are separated by the wraparound rostral. The anal plate is undivided. The pupils are vertically elliptical.

31. Saddled Leaf-nosed Snake

Phyllorhynchus browni

Abundance/Range: This is probably a common to abundant species, but as with many persistent burrowers, actual population statistics are difficult to ascertain. In the United States the range of this species is restricted to central and south central Arizona. Its Mexican range includes Sonora and the northern half of Sinaloa.

Habitat: This is a species of sandy and gravelly desert flats. It seems most common where plant associations of saguaro-creosote bush-mesquite occur, or in areas of thornscrub.

Size: Although a record size of 20 inches is mentioned, most specimens are much smaller. Typically, saddled leaf-nosed snakes range from 10 to 16 inches in length.

Saddled Leaf-nosed Snake, dark phase

Saddled Leaf-nosed Snake, light phase

Identifying features: This is one of the prettiest and most distinctively colored and patterned of our western snakes. The ground color may be white (with just the faintest blush of pink) to cream. The 17 or fewer brown dorsal blotches are darkest near their outer perimeter and fade to a lighter brown centrally. Either the dark areas or the light areas may be the widest. The belly is immaculate white. The nose is white on the sides but may be smudged with dark pigment dorsally.

Similar species: Most other snakes that occur within the range of the saddled leaf-nosed snake (including the spotted leaf-nosed snake) have a much busier, less precise dorsal pattern. The anterior edge of the rostral scale of the western hog-nosed snake is free and sharply pointed. The various rattlesnakes have tailtip rattles (unless the tailtip has been amputated), facial pits, and fragmented scales on top of their head.

ADDITIONAL SUBSPECIES

There are no longer any recognized subspecies.

32. Spotted Leaf-nosed Snake

Phyllorhynchus decurtatus

Abundance/Range: The spotted leaf-nosed snake is often seen crossing paved roadways on summer evenings and may emerge from its burrow to prowl the surface of the sand following afternoon rains. Although no definitive population studies have been completed, it seems safe to say that this is a common to abundant species. It ranges southward from extreme southwestern Utah and central eastern California, the eastern slopes of the Baja Peninsula and most of western Sonora and Sinaloa.

Habitat: This is another of the persistent burrowers in the snake fauna of the Sonoran Desert. It occurs both in sandy areas and on gravelly flats. It seems quite common where deserts host plant community associations of saguaro-creosote bush-mesquite. It is occasionally found beneath surface debris such as fallen cacti or human-generated litter.

Spotted Leaf-nosed Snake

Size: Most examples found are 11–15 inches in length. The record length is 20 inches.

Identifying features: This is a variable snake but it always has a blunt nose and an enlarged rostral scale. The ground color may be tan, buff, pinkish, or gray. The snakes having the palest colors are those from regions having the lightest colored soils. There are usually 17–40 narrow, dark-edged, brown dorsal saddles. Smaller brown spots alternate between the dorsal blotches on the sides. A narrow brown chevron-shaped band (directed anteriorly) crosses the head, encompasses the eyes, and continues to the lip. The belly is an immaculate white. The scales are in 17 rows at midbody. Females have smooth dorsal scales; those of the male are keeled. The anal plate is undivided; the pupils are vertically elliptical.

Similar species: The anterior edge of the rostral scale of the hog-nosed snake is free and strongly upturned. Gopher snakes are much larger and have strongly keeled scales. Night snakes have large dark blotches on the posterior of their head and nape. Patch-nosed snakes are striped. Rattlesnakes have the tailtip rattle (unless the tailtip has been amputated), a sensory pit on each side of the face, and fragmented scales on the top of their head.

ADDITIONAL SUBSPECIES

There are no longer any recognized subspecies.

Lyre Snakes, Genus *Trimorphodon*

The lyre snakes range widely through Middle America, but enter the United States in west Texas and the southwestern states. Except for the Texas lyre (which has dark smudges on the top of its head) these snakes are typified by a dark, lyre-shaped marking on the rear of the head. The broad head is well differentiated from the slim neck. The body is slender and supple. The lyre snakes have a vertically elliptical pupil and a lorilabial scale—a scale between the loreal and the labial.

Lyre snakes are inhabitants of scrubby deserts, rocky sides of hills and mountains, and wooded canyons. They emerge from crevices and other areas of seclusion in the evening and remain active far into the night. Although these snakes spend much time on the ground, they are fully capable of climbing rock faces, where they search crevices and fissures for their prey.

Lizards are the preferred prey of the lyre snake. These snakes are adept at extracting lizards from narrow fissures. Nestling birds and rodents and smaller snakes may also be occasionally accepted. The venom produced by this rear-fanged snake effectively overcomes ectotherms but seems less effective on endotherms. Humans have developed mild swelling, redness, and some localized sensitivity as a reaction to bites, but no lingering or serious effects. Although lyre snakes are often reluctant to bite, large examples should be handled with caution. Lyre snakes are also relatively effective constrictors.

Lyre snakes are oviparous and large females have produced 20 eggs in a clutch. More typically, the clutch size is between 5 and 12 eggs. Hatchlings are about 9 inches in length.

The scales are smooth, and in the United States these snakes have 20–24 scale rows; the anal plate may be either divided or undivided.

33. Sonoran Lyre Snake

Trimorphodon biscutatus lambda

Abundance/Range: Sonoran Lyre Snakes are secretive, but often fairly common in areas of suitable habitat. The range of this race extends southward from southeastern Nevada and southwestern Utah to far south on the Mexican mainland.

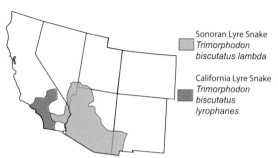

Sonoran Lyre Snake
Trimorphodon biscutatus lambda

California Lyre Snake
Trimorphodon biscutatus lyrophanes

Habitat: Although it may occasionally be found well away from rocky situations, for the most part this is a snake of rocky deserts, escarpments, boulder-strewn aridlands, and fissured outcroppings. Typical plant communities in lyre snake habitat include mesquite, creosote bush, saguaro, and ocotillo.

Size: The majority of lyre snakes encountered in the field are 24–36 inches long. The largest examples in the United States are about 4 feet long. (Tropical races attain a considerably larger size.)

Sonoran Lyre Snake

Identifying features: The ground color of the Sonoran lyre snake often closely approaches that of the rocky substrates on which the snake dwells. The ground color can vary from a rather rich brown to the palest of sandy grays. The color is usually darkest middorsally and lightest on the lower sides. There are usually about 28 light-centered, light-edged, darker dorsal blotches. Irregular small blotches are present on the lower sides. There is a well-defined lyre- or V-shaped figure present on the top of the head and the first blotch is usually noticeably elongate. The eyes have vertically elliptical pupils, and the head is much broader than the proportionately slender neck. The belly is off-white to pale yellow and is patterned with irregular dark spots. The spots are largest and most prominent at the outer edges (sides) of the ventral scutes.

Similar snakes: The gray-banded kingsnake has round pupils and lacks an intricate pattern on the top of the head. Gopher snakes have heavily keeled body scales. Glossy snakes have round pupils and a thick neck. Night snakes have elongate black spots on the sides of their neck.

ADDITIONAL SUBSPECIES

34. The most westerly race of the lyre snake is designated scientifically as *T. b. lyrophanes* and is commonly called the California Lyre Snake. This subspecies has an average of 35 dorsal blotches. Individuals from the

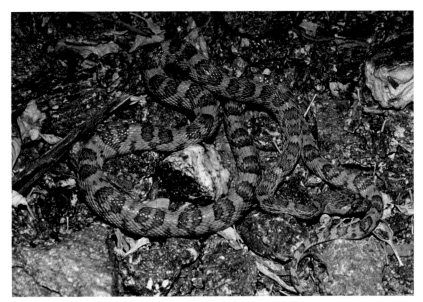

California Lyre Snake

white-sand deserts of southern California can be so pallid that the dorsal blotches are difficult to define. It ranges southward and southwestward from the vicinity of Inyo County, California, to central Baja California.

35. Texas Lyre Snake

Trimorphodon vilkinsonii

Abundance/Range: This beautiful, secretive, and nocturnal snake is rather generally distributed from Texas' Big Bend to central New Mexico, but is nowhere common.

Habitat: It is seen most often in boulder-strewn areas and rocky hillsides along the Rio Grande. It has been found both beneath rocks and beneath the flaking exfoliations of boulders. It may be active when the temperature is only in the 60s° F.

Size: Adults are usually 32 inches or less and the record size is 41 inches.

Identifying features: The Texas lyre snake is quite different in appearance from the other species in this genus. It lacks a well-defined head pattern, has fewer than 24 (some specimens have as few as 17) comparatively narrow, widely separated primary dorsal blotches, and may have a slight

Texas Lyre Snake

greenish cast to its limestone gray or earthen brown ground color. The blotches, which are often roughly diamond shaped, are narrowly outlined in darker pigment and outside of that by light pigment.

The belly is light (tan or yellowish) and bears a row of well-spaced dark spots along each outer edge.

Similar snakes: Both subspecies of the rock rattlesnakes have rattles. The gray-banded kingsnake often has some red or orange in the dorsal pattern, is banded rather than having dorsal saddles, and has round pupils.

ADDITIONAL SUBSPECIES

None.

LAMPROPELTINE SNAKES: GLOSSY, RAT, KING, GOPHER, AND LONG-NOSED SNAKES

Although not recognized by systematists, this grouping is a convenient repository for these well-known, obviously related constricting snakes. These snakes are the favorites of the world's herpetoculturists, but there is still considerably less known about the behavior of these snakes in the wild than in captivity.

All are powerful constrictors. Several species in differing genera have been known to interbreed when natural habitat partitions are removed or altered by varying modifications, or by bringing the snakes into contact in captivity. In most cases the resulting offspring are viable and breed readily. None are venomous; all are oviparous.

Glossy Snakes, Genus *Arizona*

Taxonomic note: For the last several decades, this has been treated as a monotypic genus. Currently, however, based on allopatry and comparative tail length, some taxonomists feel that the genus should be split into two species. If this occurs, the genus would contain *A. elegans* and *A. occidentalis*, the eastern long-tailed form and the western short-tailed form, respectively.

For the moment we will discuss the glossy snake as a single species. Seven variable races occur in the United States. One, the Texas glossy snake, *Arizona elegans arenicola*, occurs east of the scope of this book. Additional races may be found in Mexico.

Glossy snakes are nonvenomous, but may bite if provoked. The glossy snakes are considered relatives of the pine, gopher, and bullsnakes of the genus *Pituophis* and, like them, are oviparous. The glossy snake has non-keeled body scales in as few as 25, or as many as 35, rows, occasionally one but usually two prefrontal scales, and an undivided anal plate. The head is narrow but distinct. The glossy snake is an efficient burrower, and very secretive, indulging in surface activity, primarily after darkness has fallen, to seek its prey. Although lizards figure very prominently in the diet of these snakes, glossy snakes also prey on suitably sized rodents, ground-dwelling birds, and smaller snakes. Glossy snakes are capable of strong and sustained constriction but do not often constrict small prey items.

Glossy snakes are both crepuscular and nocturnal.

Studies have disclosed that not all female glossy snakes in wild populations reproduce every year. Conversely, an occasional captive female will double clutch in a given year, a pattern not documented in the wild. Normal clutches contain 5–12 eggs. Clutches of 3–23 eggs have been recorded. Incubation lasts for 68–80 days.

36. Kansas Glossy Snake

Arizona elegans elegans

Abundance/Range: This is a commonly encountered snake. It ranges southward from northeastern Colorado and southwestern Nebraska, through eastern New Mexico and northern and western Texas, well into northeastern Mexico.

Habitat: The Kansas glossy snake is common in open habitats. It may be found in prairies, plains, open deserts, and desert scrub, along rocky washes and river

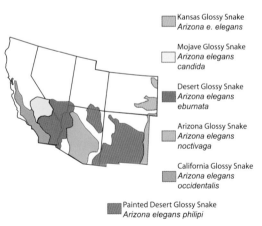

Kansas Glossy Snake
Arizona e. elegans

Mojave Glossy Snake
Arizona elegans candida

Desert Glossy Snake
Arizona elegans eburnata

Arizona Glossy Snake
Arizona elegans noctivaga

California Glossy Snake
Arizona elegans occidentalis

Painted Desert Glossy Snake
Arizona elegans philipi

floodplains, and in chaparral and grasslands. It may be found along the edges of wooded areas, but tends to shun densely treed areas. It prefers areas with soil of loose consistency into which it can easily burrow. Be-

Kansas Glossy Snake, normal phase

Kansas Glossy Snake, striped phase

sides burrows of its own making, the glossy snake may use the burrows of rodents or other desert creatures, and may also be found beneath natural and human-generated surface debris.

Size: Although rare examples may approach 6 feet in length, most glossy snakes are 30–42 inches long. Males are noticeably the smaller sex in this snake species. Hatchlings vary between 9½ and 12½ inches in length.

Identifying features: This is a wide-blotched, long-tailed race. It has a long tail and a rather dark ground color that varies from tan to pale brown. The dark-edged blotches are deeper brown. The average dorsal blotch count is 53 (39–69). The scales are smooth and in 29 or 31 rows.

The blotches are wider than the lighter areas of ground color that separate them. There are usually 2 preocular scales on each side.

Similar species: The gopher snakes and bullsnakes have very strongly keeled body scales. The various rat snakes have weakly keeled middorsal scales and a divided anal plate. Night snakes and lyre snakes have vertically elliptical pupils. Juvenile racers have a divided anal plate.

ADDITIONAL SUBSPECIES

37. The Mojave Glossy Snake, *A. e. candida*, ranges from Inyo County, California, eastward to the Death Valley area of western Nevada and westward and southward throughout much of the western Mojave Desert in California. It may be found in open deserts, desert scrub, along rocky washes and river floodplains, chaparral and grasslands.

This is one of the light-colored desert races of glossy snake. The ground color is a light sandy tan to grayish tan. The 53–73 (average 63) dark blotches are buff, olive buff, or olive tan, and are edged anteriorly and posteriorly with a darker olive and noticeably narrower than the light spaces that separate them. A series of small lateral blotches alternate with the dorsal blotches. The smooth scales are in 27 or fewer scale rows. The venter is a pale sandy olive to light buff with an olive blush. Because of its proportionate narrowness, the head looks elongate. This race has 2 preocular scales and a proportionately short tail.

Mojave Glossy Snake

Desert Glossy Snake

38. In keeping with its aridland habitat, the Desert Glossy Snake, *A. e. eburnata*, has an overall pale coloration. The ground color is a sandy cream, the poorly contrasting, olive brown, dorsal blotches are weakly edged with slightly darker pigment anteriorly and posteriorly. The body scales are in 27 or fewer rows. This race usually has only one preocular scale. The narrow dorsal blotches average 68 (53–85) and are narrower than the width of the ground color that separates them. This race has a short tail. This subspecies ranges southward from southern Nevada and adjacent southwestern Utah and northeastern Arizona, through eastern California, and into northeastern Baja California.

39. The Arizona Glossy Snake, *A. e. noctivaga,* has a ground color of tan to light reddish brown. The dorsal blotches are deeper brown and narrowly edged anteriorly and posteriorly with darker pigment. The midbody scale rows of this race may vary from 25 to 29, but are often 27. It may have 1 or 2 preocular scales. The dorsal blotches are about the same width as, but may be slightly wider than, the light areas of ground color that separate them. There are 66 (53–77) dorsal blotches, on average. The venter is pale and unmarked. The lower labial scales usually lack dark markings. The tail is comparatively short. This race occurs in desert chaparral and brushlands from western and southern Arizona to Sinaloa, Mexico.

Arizona Glossy Snake

40. The California Glossy Snake, *A. e. occidentalis*, is a variable, but usually relatively dark snake dorsally. It has a ground color of olive tan to olive brown and dark-edged blotches of deep brown. This race also has dark markings on the lower labial scales and on the outer edges (sides) of the ventral scutes. There are 27 scale rows, 2 preoculars, and a short tail. The

California Glossy Snake

dorsal blotches are about equal in width to the light areas of ground color between them and average 63 (51–75) in number. This subspecies ranges southward from the San Francisco Bay area through much of western California to northwestern Baja California.

41. The ground color of the Painted Desert Glossy Snake, *A. e. philipi*, is a pretty buff. The saddles are a dark-edged, darker brown. On this long-tailed race, the scales are normally in 27 (rarely 25 or 29) rows. There are an average of 64 (53–80) dorsal blotches. Expect this race from southeastern Utah, through much of central and western New Mexico, to extreme northeastern Sonora and northern Chihuahua, Mexico.

Painted Desert Glossy Snake

Desert Rat Snakes, Genus *Bogertophis*

This bitypic genus contains big-eyed, desert and rocky savanna, and riparian scrubland snakes. They are capable of constricting prey, but may not always do so. Both species are egg-layers. Some researchers consider the two snakes in this genus more closely allied to the bull and gopher snakes than to the rat snake genus *Pantherophis* (formerly *Elaphe*) from which *Bogertophis* was only recently separated. These nonvenomous snakes seldom bite. The head is broad, somewhat flattened, and distinct from the slender neck. A row of subocular scales separates the eyes from the upper labials (lip scales). The body scales are weakly keeled, arranged in 31–35

rows, and the anal plate is divided. Both are primarily of Mexican distribution; however, one, the Trans-Pecos rat snake, is of regular occurrence
in the United States, being very well known in west Texas and in south
central New Mexico. The main range of the more westerly Baja rat snake
is the southern Baja Peninsula. A very few specimens have been found in
northern Baja and adjacent California.

Although nervous, these nocturnal snakes do not seem inclined to bite.
They are oviparous, probably laying only a single clutch of up to 12 eggs
annually in the wild. Well-fed captives may double clutch. Reproductively
active males are known to fight savagely, causing rather severe, bloody
wounds to one another. Egg deposition occurs in June, July, and August.
Following an incubation period of 62–75 (rarely to more than 100) days,
the hatchlings emerge in late August, September, October, November, or
rarely, early December.

These snakes eat both rodents and lizards but show a preference for
prey items of comparatively small size. Wild specimens have regurgitated
bats, unidentified rodents, and iguanian lizards.

42. Baja California Rat Snake

Bogertophis rosaliae

Abundance/Range: This snake is rare in the United States but
well known on the Baja Peninsula, where it ranges southward
along the eastern slopes to Cabo San Lucas at the southern tip.
In the United States it seems restricted to Imperial County,
California.
Habitat: Rock- and boulder-strewn regions of arid scrub are
home to this snake. It has been found near desert streams and
springs.
Size: Although rather slender, this interesting rat snake attains a
length of 3–4 feet. The record size is 58 inches.
Identifying features: The Baja California rat snake has a slender, supple
body and a broad head that is distinct from the neck. The eyes are protu-
berant but not overly large. A row of subocular scales separates the bottom of the eye from the supralabial scales. The body scales are usually in
31, 33, or 35 rows at midbody. The lateral scales are smooth, the dorsolat-

Baja California Rat Snake

eral scales are usually smooth, but the middorsal scales are usually very weakly keeled. The keels may be difficult to see. The anal plate is divided.

Adults may be reddish brown, silver gray, olive gray, or olive yellow dorsally and are paler below. Hatchlings look delicately translucent, especially ventrally. Juveniles usually have a ground color of olive yellow, olive orange, to olive gray. A vague, paler vertebral stripe with well-separated, pale partial bands extending downward is present. The markings, best defined anteriorly, fade quickly with growth.

Similar species: None within the range of this species.

ADDITIONAL SUBSPECIES

None.

43. Trans-Pecos Rat Snake

Bogertophis subocularis subocularis

Abundance/Range: Rather common in Texas' Big Bend region and south of the international border, the Trans-Pecos rat snake is considered relatively rare in its limited New Mexico range.

Trans-Pecos Rat Snake

Habitat: Sparsely vegetated, boulder-strewn Chihuahuan desert habitats are the home of this snake. It is often found near stock tanks, along intermittent streams, or in riparian situations.

Size: Occasional specimens of the Trans-Pecos rat snake may measure 5½ feet in length. Most, however, are considerably smaller, measuring only 3–4½ feet. Although very large examples actually seem to "chunk up," the trans-Pecos rat snake is normally a slender serpent, particularly the hatchlings.

Identifying features: This big-eyed (it has even been referred to as "bug-eyed") constrictor occurs in several color morphs. The ground color may vary from olive gray to olive green in the north to straw yellow or yellow orange in the south and east A small percentage of the easternmost specimens (from the vicinity of Texas' Christmas Mountains) have a greenish yellow to blonde ground color. The Christmas Mountain aberrancies also have an aberrant pattern.

Typically, the dorsal pattern consists of two wide, parallel, black dorsolateral stripes. At a point anterior to midbody the stripes are joined by crossbars and become broken into the characteristic H's. White markings may show interstitially, especially where the crossbars of the H join the dorsolateral stripes. A series of lateral blotches, often poorly defined, is usually visible on each side.

The aberrant (blonde) Christmas Mountain examples have a dorsal pattern consisting of simple, light-centered, darker dorsal saddles and a single vertebral neck stripe. If lateral blotches are present on this phase, they are vague at best.

In all phases, the dorsal surface of the head is unpatterned, and a row of subocular scales separates the eye from the supralabial scales. The dorsal scales are in 31–35 rows. The lateral rows are not keeled, the dorsolateral rows may be very weakly keeled, and the dorsal scale rows are weakly keeled; the anal plate is divided.

Similar snakes: None within the range of this species.

ADDITIONAL SUBSPECIES

None in the United States. The only other race, *Bogertophis subocularis amplinota*, occurs in southern Coahuila and Durango, Mexico.

American Rat Snakes, Genus *Pantherophis*

Taxonomic note: Until very recently these snakes were in the genus *Elaphe*. It has recently been suggested that they be removed from the genus *Pantherophis* and placed with the gopher and bull snakes in the genus *Pituophis*. This proposed reclassification has not been well accepted.

The Great Plains rat snake is considered a full species, *Pantherophis emoryi*, by some researchers.

Although this genus is abundantly represented in the eastern United States, in the American west it is represented by only a single species, the Great Plains rat snake, the westerly representative of the corn snake clan.

When adult, the snakes of this genus have weakly keeled dorsal and dorsolateral scales and unkeeled lateral scales. The juveniles of all lack scale keels. The number of scale rows varies both by species and individually. The Great Plains rat snake has 27–29 rows of scales. The anal plate is divided.

If looked at in cross-section, the rat snakes would be seen to be rounded on top, to have weakly convex sides, and to have a flattened venter. Rat snakes are agile climbers that can ascend virtually straight up a tree with only moderately rough bark and can even ascend smooth-barked trees (though with more difficulty) if they choose.

Rat snakes are often drawn to barnyard and ranch settings by the proliferation of rodents.

The American rat snakes are very powerful constrictors. Juvenile rat snakes usually feed on small lizards and treefrogs, while the adults consume rodents, rabbits, and some birds. If frightened or carelessly restrained, these snakes may bite, but many don't. They are nonvenomous. They are crepuscular during cool weather but nocturnal during the summer.

All American rat snakes are oviparous. The Great Plains rat snake has been known to lay up to 25 eggs in a clutch (8–16 is more normal) and they may occasionally double clutch. Hatchlings, 10–12½ inches long, emerge after about 60 days of incubation.

44. Great Plains Rat Snake

Pantherophis guttata emoryi

Abundance/Range: This common, wide-ranging rat snake occurs in our central and western states and northeastern Mexico. In harsh regions it is locally distributed. In the American west, the Great Plains rat snake may be found in eastern New Mexico, southeastern Colorado, and in a disjunct population in central western Colorado and adjacent Utah. A single record exists from the extreme northeastern corner of Utah.

☒ Corn Snake, *Pantherophis g. guttata*

☐ Great Plains Rat Snake, *Pantherophis g. emoryi*

Habitat: The Great Plains rat snake inhabits a variety of habitats, but it is more dependent on a source of water than species such as the trans-Pecos rat snake are. Although it wanders widely, somewhere within its range there is usually a spring, stock tank, stream, pond, or lake to which it will return when necessary. It is often drawn to the vicinity of human habitations, not only for the water they provide and the rodents to be found there, but also because human-generated surface debris provides ample areas for seclusion. Rock- or boulder- strewn areas in the vicinity of watercourses also provide excellent natural habitat. Fissures in canyon sides, escarpments, talus, the entrance and twilight zones of caves and mines are all

Great Plains Rat Snake, Texas locale

Great Plains Rat Snake, Utah locale

habitats utilized. Water availability due to irrigation practices has allowed the Great Plains rat snake to expand its range in some areas.

Size: The Great Plains rat snake seldom exceeds 4½ feet in length and the record length is only five feet one quarter inch.

Identifying features: This subspecies is the least colorful member of the corn snake complex. The Great Plains rat snake is often a pleasing combination of brown on gray. However, this snake is variable, both inter- and intra-populationally. The ground color can vary from a mid-gray to an olive brown, and both the dorsal saddles and the lateral blotches may be a light olive gray, olive brown, medium brown, or rich chocolate brown. The saddles are often narrowly edged with darker pigment.

There is a dark spearpoint atop the head, and a dark bar runs diagonally upward through each eye from the jawline; they converge on the top of the snout. The head markings may fade with advancing age.

The belly may be prominently checkered, diffusely checkered, or immaculate. The underside of the tail may or may not have dark stripes. There may be pockets of specimens with an unpatterned belly interspersed among those with a prominently checkerboarded belly. This appears to be a trait of individuals, rather than of populations.

Similar species: The blotched young of racers have smooth scales and lack the spearpoint design on the top of the head. Glossy snakes have smooth scales and a single anal plate. Bull and gopher snakes have a vertically oriented, wraparound rostral scale and heavily keeled dorsal and lateral scales.

ADDITIONAL SUBSPECIES/COMMENTS

Although we have included it as a race of the corn snake, some taxonomists consider the Great Plains rat snake a full species and designate it *P. emoryi*. There is a northern race (*emoryi*) and a southern race (*meahllmorum*). If valid, the same subspecific designations may be made (as they once were) while retaining the Great Plains rat snake in the species *guttata*. Such nomenclature will then continue to show the obvious relationship of the Great Plains rat snake to the corn snake.

44a. The Corn Snake, *Pantherophis guttata guttata*, is native to the eastern United States. It is, however, bred in vast numbers in captivity for the pet industry, and escapees or examples deliberately released are now being found in many regions. Feral corn snakes are most common in cities but have been found in areas as remote as Scissors Crossing, California. The corn snake is of very variable color, but usually has an orange or gray ground color and red dorsal saddles. Albinos and about thirty other designer colors and patterns have been developed.

Corn Snake

Neotropical Rat Snakes, Genus *Senticolis*

Based on biochemical differences, as well as on differences in scale structure, osteology, and hemipenial morphology, this genus was erected in 1987 by Dowling and Fries. The genus contains only the single species and several races of *S. triaspis*. These snakes are collectively termed the Neotropical rat snakes.

The genus is represented in the United States only in the mountains of extreme southeastern Arizona by *S. t. intermedia*. The southernmost extreme of the range is northern Costa Rica.

45. Northern Green Rat Snake

Senticolis triaspis intermedia

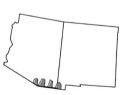

Abundance/Range: This is not an uncommon snake, but in the United States it is at the northernmost periphery of its range. It may be expected in many of the mountain ranges extending northward from Sonora into eastern Pima County, Santa Cruz County, and Cochise County, Arizona, as well as in western Hidalgo County, New Mexico.

Habitat: Look for this species among boulders along streams in forested mountain canyons in extreme southeastern Arizona and immediately ad-

Northern Green Rat Snake

jacent New Mexico. It may also disperse into drier habitats. It is most commonly encountered in the spring of the year, during periods of lowering barometric pressure, or as it moves about on summer evenings. It is associated with relatively high elevations (to more than 6,500 feet). Specimens have been found resting by day in low brush, from one to five feet above the ground, but are also known to spend much time secluded in rock crevices and beneath boulders. They may remain inactive for periods of more than a week. It is probable that this snake is primarily terrestrial, but it is fully capable of climbing agilely. These snakes seem most active during periods of lowering (or low) barometric pressure, such as that which accompanies the advent of storm systems. They are active at moderate temperatures throughout the warm months of the year.

Size: This is a slender species that often reaches 3–4¼ feet in length, and occasionally attains, or barely exceeds, 5 feet. Females are noticeably the larger sex.

Identifying features: Like many rat snakes, the green rat snake undergoes considerable ontogenetic change. The hatchlings have a ground color of olive tan to tan or light olive brown. About 70 darker dorsal blotches are present from the nape to the vent. These may be in the form of saddles, or offset vertebrally into a checkerboard pattern. The blotches fade rather quickly with growth, but may occasionally be faintly visible well into adulthood. Normally colored adult snakes are an unmarked olive to a rather bright green dorsally, and have an immaculate white to off-white or yellowish venter. The scales on the flanks are smooth, but dorsal scales are weakly keeled. The scales of Arizona specimens are in 31–39 rows and the anal plate is divided. The snout is rather long and squared when viewed from above. This snake is often short tempered, but bites are not of serious consequence.

Similar species: Adults of this snake are unlikely to be mistaken for any other snake species in their range. Geographic distribution and the weakly keeled dorsal scales differentiate this greenish snake from the smaller, more brightly colored, smooth-scaled green snake. The strongly blotched young might be mistaken for a lyre snake, a Great Plains rat snake, a racer, or a whipsnake. However, the lyre snake has a prominent intricate pattern on the top of its head and vertically elliptical pupils, while the head pattern of the green rat snake is less well defined and its pupils are round. The Great Plains rat snake does not occur within the range of the green rat snake. Racers and whipsnakes have smooth dorsal scales.

ADDITIONAL SUBSPECIES

Two additional subspecies occur south of the international boundary.

Kingsnakes and Milk Snakes, Genus *Lampropeltis*

As currently understood, there are five species of milk snakes and kingsnakes in the western United States. These are the common kingsnakes, *L. getula* ssp. (3 races); the Sonoran mountain kingsnakes, *L. pyromelana* ssp. (2 races); the California Mountain kingsnakes, *L. zonata* (now not subspeciated but formerly with 7 races); the milk snakes, *L. triangulum* ssp. (4 races); and the gray-banded kingsnake, *L. alterna*.

The scales of all members of this genus are smooth and appear shiny and polished. All species and subspecies have undivided anal plates.

The snakes of this genus are powerful constrictors noted for their occasional ophiophagous (even cannibalistic) tendencies. Kingsnakes and milk snakes seem immune, or at least very resistant, to the venoms of the various venomous snakes with which they share their habitats. They also eat lizards, turtles and their eggs, amphibians, small mammals, and ground nesting birds.

Kingsnakes and milk snakes vary greatly in disposition. Some will allow indiscriminate handling without any show of temper while others will strike and bite at the smallest disturbance. While being held some of these snakes may push your hand gently with the snout, then slowly open their mouth and bite and chew. These snakes are nonvenomous. Besides biting, milk snakes and kingsnakes may void and smear feces and musk on the hand and arm of the person holding it.

The various races of the common kingsnakes have dark ground colors, while the gray-banded kingsnake and the various milk snakes can be clad in very brilliant colors.

Some of the milk snakes are remarkable mimics of the venomous coral snakes, but in the United States the two have the ring sequence arranged differently. The coral snakes of the United States have the two warning colors of a traffic signal—the yellow for caution and the red for stop—touching. The harmless milk snakes have the two caution colors separated by black.

All species in this genus are oviparous. Females may have one or occasionally two rather small clutches of proportionately large eggs annually.

The incubation period is 45–70 days. Hatchlings vary in size according to the size of the adults. The smaller milk snakes may be only 5 or 6 inches long at hatching, while the larger kingsnakes may near a foot in length. Hatchlings of all are very like the adults in appearance but are usually paler, and if speckled or of a tricolored species, the light flecks or rings are usually off-white rather than yellow.

Milk snakes and gray-banded kingsnakes are primarily nocturnal, while the other kingsnakes are more diurnal.

Kingsnakes and Relatives

I was just coming into the city of Borrego Springs, California, when the headlights disclosed a wriggling snake in midroad. Initially I thought it to be a California kingsnake, *Lampropeltis getula californiae*, and I opted to simply drive on by. But as I passed the snake I glanced at it again and it didn't look quite right for a Cal king. It looked to have an awfully pointed nose. So I skidded to a stop and hopped out. This proved to be a good decision, for despite being clad in the black and white bands so typical of California kingsnakes of the region, the snake did indeed have a pointed nose. It was a bicolored (or at least mostly bicolored) long-nosed snake, *Rhinocheilus lecontei*.

continued

Long-noses are common and pretty desert snakes, but unlike the one now illuminated in the flashlight beam, most of them have, in addition to the black and white, a variable amount of strawberry red. They are definitely a tricolored snake and a very pretty tricolored snake at that.

It was on the same road a couple of nights later that I did see a California kingsnake, the real McCoy this time. I was motoring through a lengthy road cut with a car close behind. I'm always reluctant to stop under these circumstances. So I slowed to allow the following car to pass (which it didn't). I slowed some more. Red and blue lights started flashing from the car behind and I pulled over and stopped. It was a California Department of Game and Fish Officer. He was brusque at first, but when he learned I was looking for snakes and had checked my licenses, we were soon comparing notes about things we had seen during our night drives over these roads.

A few minutes of this and he was on his way again. He left first and was soon lost to sight, but about two miles down the road, I saw the flashing lights again. As I slowed to pass him, he waved me over. As I left my car he pointed to the side of the road—lying partially coiled was a large, pretty, banded California kingsnake.

MEXICANA COMPLEX KINGSNAKES

46. Gray-banded Kingsnake

Lampropeltis alterna

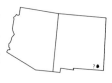

Abundance/Range: Once thought to be rare, it is now known that, in Texas, gray-banded kingsnakes are actually common snakes that are masters at evading detection.

They may, however, actually be uncommon in New Mexico, where they are a peripheral species.

Habitat: In New Mexico this kingsnake occurs, as far as is known, only in and along canyons in the southernmost regions of Eddy and Otero counties. It is a rock-crevice dwelling snake. In Texas this is a species of rocky desert flats, fissured escarpments and canyonsides, road cuts, and

Gray-banded Kingsnake

other such Chihuahuan Desert habitats. Most specimens seen by casual observers are in the process of crossing paved trans-desert roads, rather late at night. Hobbyists hunt road cuts and canyons with powerful lights for this coveted species.

Size: This is a moderate-sized kingsnake. Adults are typically between 26 and 40 inches in length. The record size is 57¾ inches long—just 2¼ inches shy of 5 feet! Hatchlings are between 9½ and 12½ inches in length. Hatchlings are quite slender, but gray-bands bulk up some with growth. However, they never appear stout.

Identifying features: Although only the black banded, gray, alterna phase has been found in New Mexico, it is possible that the blairi phase may eventually also be found.

As indicated by both the specific name and the hobbyist vernacular, the alterna phase has broken black bands alternating with complete black bands on a gray ground color. If any orange pigment is present on this phase, it is usually restricted to the neck and the tail.

The blairi phase of the gray-banded kingsnake is more variable. The ground color may vary from dark gray to light gray. The dark crossbands may be narrow or wide, mostly black, with red or orange centers dorsally, and with white edging, or mostly red (or orange) with narrow black edging, and with each band bordered anteriorly and posteriorly with a narrow pale ash or white edging.

The ventral coloration is gray with black blotches and spots. The dark coloration may occasionally predominate.

The body scales are smooth, in 25 rows, and the anal plate is not divided.

Although adults feed opportunistically on both lizards and suitably sized rodents (especially nestlings), in most cases it is lizards that predominate in the diet. These snakes seem particularly adept at finding sleeping diurnal lizards that have sought nighttime refuge beneath the rocks and in the fissures and crevices through which the snakes prowl by night.

Some hatchlings and juveniles will accept only lizards as prey.

Similar species: The black-banded alterna phase is quite similar in color to the banded rock rattlesnake; however, the kingsnake lacks the telltale rattle and is of more slender build than the rattler. Lyre snakes are slender, tend toward a browner coloration, but have a vertically elliptical pupil (that of the kingsnake is round). There are no other snakes similar in appearance to the red-saddled "blairi" phase.

ADDITIONAL SUBSPECIES

Although it is still considered a component of the *Lampropeltis mexicana* complex, as currently understood, the gray-banded kingsnake has no subspecies.

Comments: This kingsnake has captured the interest of herpetoculturists, and hundreds (perhaps thousands) of locality-specific hatchlings are produced by dozens (perhaps hundreds) of hobbyists each year. For many years the saddled "blairi" phase gray-banded kingsnakes were assigned a different subspecific name than the banded "alterna" phase examples. For pattern-phase identification purposes, hobbyists still continue to refer to these animals simply as "blairi" and "alterna."

COMMON KINGSNAKES

47. California Kingsnake

Lampropeltis getula californiae

Abundance/Range: This is a common, even abundant, snake in suitable habitats. It is remarkably adaptable, and persists in some numbers not only in wilderness areas, but in farmlands, ranches, and even some brushy suburban areas. It ranges southward from southwestern Oregon and southwestern Colorado, throughout California and most of Arizona, to northern Sonora and the southernmost tip of the Baja Peninsula.

California Kingsnake
Lampropeltis getula californiae

Mexican Black Kingsnake
Lampropeltis getula nigrita

Desert Kingsnake
Lampropeltis getula splendida

Habitat: The California kingsnake may be encountered in myriad habitats. It may be found in desert, semidesert, areas of brush, grasslands, pastures and meadows, canyons, marshes, swamps, and other such habitat. It seems most common where there is access to either natural or artificial water holes, or in riparian situations, but it may also be encountered far from standing water.

California Kingsnake, black and white barred phase

California Kingsnake, brown and white barred phase

California Kingsnake, black and white striped phase

Size: Smaller than many of the extralimital eastern races, the California kingsnake seldom exceeds a total length of 4 feet, and lengths between 2½ and 3½ feet are far more common.

Identifying features: This is an extremely variable subspecies. The most common color phase has a deep brown to black ground color prominently marked with narrow to wide cream to pure white crossbands that widen ventrolaterally. In some areas a striped phase occurs. This beautiful morph has a vertebral stripe 2 or 3 scales wide, usually entire but sometimes broken, on a chocolate brown ground color. The lateral scales often have some degree of white tipping. Intermediates between the two phases are known. A "desert phase" has jet black ground color and narrow, stark white bands. The banded phase has a dark and white belly; the striped phase has a chocolate belly. The California kingsnake has a large amount of white on its snout and white labial scales. It has 23 rows of nonkeeled body scales. Hatchlings and juveniles are very much like adults in coloration.

Similar snakes: There are few snakes that can be mistaken for the California kingsnake. Occasional specimens of the California mountain kingsnake may lack red bands, but their white rings do not broaden ventrolaterally. Some long-nosed snakes also lack red. However, they have many nondivided subcaudal scales.

Comments: Albino California kingsnakes are well documented in the wild. Thousands of California kingsnakes in all of their natural patterns and colors, as well as many very unnatural ones, are now bred annually in captivity for the pet trade. Some of these are white with black or chocolate stripes. Others have a ground color of lavender or cream. Besides their natural variability, strangely patterned and hued California kingsnakes escaped from or released by hobbyists are often found.

ADDITIONAL SUBSPECIES

The common kingsnake group is represented to the east of our range by numerous subspecies. In the west two additional subspecies occur. These two, the Mexican black kingsnake and the desert kingsnake, are discussed below.

48. The Mexican Black Kingsnake, *L. g. nigrita*, enters the United States from its Mexican stronghold only in extreme southeastern Arizona. It is also an arid and semiarid-land race. Where its range abuts that of the California or the desert kingsnake, intergrades are well documented. Many examples are shiny dark brown to black, with few, if any, yellow markings, and often no evidence of a dorsal chain, dorsal banding, or dorsal striping; however, those found in the United States often have a tiny light dot on each lateral scale. If a pattern *is* present, it is invariably most evident on the sides. Hatchlings tend to show more yellow and stronger evidence

Mexican Black Kingsnake

of a pattern than adults, but usually become darker with each successive shedding. (There is also an eastern race of kingsnake designated as the black kingsnake, *L. g. nigra*. The two should not be confused.)

49. The Desert Kingsnake, *L. g. splendida*, has a variable and intricate patterning. The ground color varies from brown to black. The dark sides are usually prominently speckled with yellow, or yellowish cream. A series of narrow yellow(ish) crossbands divides the dark back into a variable number of saddles. There is much yellow on the labial scales and head of this snake. In the United States, the desert kingsnake ranges westward

Desert Kingsnake

from central Texas, over much of southern New Mexico, to the south-eastern corner of Arizona. Disjunct populations occur in northern New Mexico, and intergrade populations in southeastern Colorado and south-western Colorado (see comments, above). Although well adapted to arid and semiarid conditions, desert kingsnakes seem most common where surface water is always, or nearly always, available.

SONORAN MOUNTAIN KINGSNAKES

50. Arizona Mountain Kingsnake

Lampropeltis pyromelana pyromelana

Abundance/Range: Although this snake is not uncommon, its canyon homelands are not easily accessed. The Arizona mountain kingsnake (with which the Huachuca Mountain kingsnake is now synonymized) occurs in many of the mountains of southwestern New Mexico, southeastern and central Arizona, and north central Mexico.

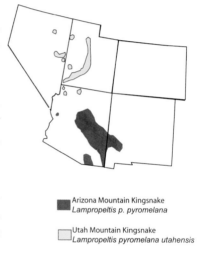

■ Arizona Mountain Kingsnake
Lampropeltis p. pyromelana

□ Utah Mountain Kingsnake
Lampropeltis pyromelana utahensis

Habitat: This is a snake of rocky, forested, montane canyons. It seeks solitude in creviced escarpments and beneath jumbled rocks and fallen logs. It prefers habitats with an ample water supply. Besides canyons, these king-snakes may also be found at the edges of rock-strewn mountain meadows, along mountain streams, and at the foot of talus slides. Although they have been found as low as 3,000 feet in elevation, these snakes are most common at elevations of from 4,500 to 9,000 feet.

Size: These snakes are adult at 20–30 inches, with a record size of 44 inches documented.

Identifying features: Range, and the beautiful and precisely delineated pattern of red, black, and white rings will identify this medium-sized kingsnake. White body rings may vary in number between 37 and 61 and do not widen ventrally. Most brilliantly colored when young, this snake darkens with advancing age, and black pigment may suffuse and replace the red along the center of the back. The belly is paler than the dorsum,

Arizona Mountain Kingsnake

and the red predominates. The black markings may be broken or offset midventrally. The snout is white. There are 10 lower labial scales and usually 23 scale rows at midbody.

Similar species: The banded sand snake and the shovel-nosed snake are very small, have saddles, not rings, of color, and are not associated with montane canyons. Milk snakes have the white rings expanded at the bottom. The long-nosed snake has many rows of subcaudal scales in a single row.

ADDITIONAL SUBSPECIES

51. The Utah Mountain Kingsnake, *L. p. infralabialis*, differs from the nominate form only in having 9 rather than 10 lower labial scales. This subspecies ranges northward in various mountain ranges, from extreme north central Arizona, to central Utah and central eastern Nevada.

An extralimital race, *L. p. knoblochi*, bearing a more pastel red and a reduced amount of black pigment, occurs in the Sierra Madre Occidental of northern Mexico.

Utah Mountain Kingsnake. Photo by Gerold C. Merker

MILK SNAKES

52. New Mexican Milk Snake

Lampropeltis triangulum celaenops

Abundance/Range: Although this snake is often thought to be rare, this does not seem to actually be the case. Surface activity is instigated by rains, and (apparently) to a lesser degree by the passage of dry fronts that cause a falling barometric pressure. The New Mexican milk snake occurs in a large but difficult to delineate area that begins in western Val Verde County, Texas, and extends westward and northward in a narrow swath along the Rio Grande, through New Mexico to extreme southeastern Arizona and south central and southwestern Colorado. It may be found from sea level to elevations of more than 7,000 feet.

Habitat: The New Mexican milk snake is most often found in rock- and boulder-strewn, riparian areas, but wanders far out into semidesert and desert scrublands as well. It is also found in grasslands and forested areas, and in sandhills. As do other subspecies

New Mexican Milk Snake
Lampropeltis triangulum celaenops

Central Plains Milk Snake
Lampropeltis t. gentilis

Pale Milk Snake
Lampropeltis t. multistriata

Utah Milk Snake
Lampropeltis t. taylori

New Mexican Milk Snake, West Texas locale

New Mexican Milk Snake, southeastern Arizona locale

of this wide-ranging snake, the New Mexican milk snake utilizes both natural and human-generated surface debris for hiding, including rocks and fallen tree trunks as well as boards, newspaper, etc. Though fully capable of burrowing, this snake readily enters the burrows of lizards and small mammals.

Size: This is one of the smaller races of the milk snake. Most specimens found are between 14 and 18 inches in overall length, but examples to 30 inches have been documented.

Identifying features: The New Mexican milk snake is one of the more brightly colored of the western milk snakes. Although not truly scarlet, the wide red rings are bright and usually lack black tipping. The chalk white to yellow rings (which are widest near the belly) are next widest, and although black tipping is present, the color still contrasts sharply with the red and black. The black rings are narrowest. The black and the white bands completely encircle the body (extending across the belly) but the red bands are often discontinuous on the belly. The black bands usually expand middorsally and may (rarely) interrupt the red banding vertebrally. The nose is primarily black, but usually bears some white spotting. There are 21 scale rows.

Similar snakes: On the coral snake, the two caution colors, red and yellow, are touching each other. Banded sand snakes and shovel-nosed snakes have saddles of color (not rings). Both have a white (yellowish) belly. The Sonoran mountain kingsnake has a white snout, and its white rings do not become wider near the belly.

ADDITIONAL SUBSPECIES

53. The Central Plains Milk Snake, *L. t. gentilis*, is another small and beautiful tricolored snake. Adults are usually between 18 and 24 inches in total length; the record size is 36 inches.

This subspecies has somewhat faded red bands (red, orange red to orange) of almost the same width as the white (or pale gray) bands. The

Central Plains Milk Snake

20–40 red bands are separated from the white by narrower bands of black. The black bands and the white bands encircle the body, but the red bands are usually interrupted middorsally by black pigment. The scales are in 19–21 rows. The snout is white but the scale sutures are often black. In our area, this snake occurs only in the eastern half of Colorado. From there it ranges eastward to central southern Nebraska and northern Texas. Although seldom seen and apparently rare in some locales, it is quite common in other areas. This is a secretive creature that may be found in many different types of habitats, including rocky hillsides, riparian settings, prairies, and canyons. It is fully capable of burrowing, but often chooses to secrete itself beneath rocks and surface debris or in the burrows of lizards or small mammals. It occurs from near sea level to elevations of more than 8,000 feet.

54. The Pale Milk Snake, *L. t. multistriata*, is the most northerly in distribution of the four western races of milk snake. This snake prefers open rocky woodlands, rocky prairies, and escarpments, where it secludes itself beneath logs, in stumps, behind loosened bark, and under rocks and other such ground surface litter. It ranges northwestward from extreme northeastern Colorado and southern Nebraska to central Montana.

Adults of this race normally measure between 16 and 26 inches but specimens of 30 inches have been documented.

Pale Milk Snake

Typically, this is the palest of the milk snakes. The light bars are gray(ish) rather than white or yellow, the black is reduced in quantity and the 22–38 red bands are muted to orange red or dusty red. The top of the head is dark, and the snout is whitish with orangish overtones and scattered dark markings. The bands do not completely encircle the body, leaving the midventral area a (usually) unpatterned light gray.

The body scales are smooth and usually in 19 rows. The anal plate is undivided.

55. Very little is known about the natural history of the Utah Milk Snake, *L. t. taylori*. This, the westernmost of the milk snake subspecies, is found in western central Colorado, over much of Utah to the east and south of the Great Salt Lake, and southward in the mountains to central Arizona. This snake has been found to approximately 6,000 feet in elevation.

This is a secretive little snake that, over most of its range, is happened across mostly by accident. It seldom bites, but if provoked sufficiently it will assume a defensive S and may even strike. Like other king and milk snakes, this race will vibrate its tail when nervous. It has 23–34 dull, but definite red saddles (not rings) that are often narrower than either the black or white (to pale gray) fields. The black bands may also be interrupted ventrally, leaving the belly predominantly grayish in color. The pattern of this little milk snake is well defined, but not precise. The scales

Utah Milk Snake

in both the red and the white fields have some degree of dark tipping. The nose is white with dark scale sutures and sometimes a pale orange blush.

56. California Mountain Kingsnake

Lampropeltis zonata

Taxonomic note: Traditionally this snake has been divided into seven subspecies; however, because the defining subspecific characteristics are so nebulous, no subspecies are recognized as of 2007. We acknowledge this reassessment but show the former subspecies as pattern phases. The body scales are smooth, in 21 or 23 rows at mid-body, and the anal plate is entire.

Abundance/Range: Of spotty distribution, this beautiful and variable kingsnake ranges southward from south central Washington to Baja California. It may be common in some areas but rare in others.

Habitat: From sea level to elevated mountain fastnesses, from moist wooded canyons to chaparral—if the desert is excluded, this snake may be considered a habitat generalist. It seems most common and most generally distributed in moist coniferous woodlands, but may also be encountered with some regularity in more sharply drained areas. Deeply creviced escarpments and outcrops, decomposing logs, and a permanent, or semipermanent, stream enhance habitats. This snake is adept at secreting itself in the gathered

Santa Helena Mountain Kingsnake
Lampropeltis zonata

Sierra Mountain Kingsnake

Coast Mountain Kingsnake

San Bernardino Mountain Kingsnake

San Diego Mountain Kingsnake

Apparent intergrades

duff on forest floors, beneath surface rocks, and in rock and earthen fissures. It also occurs in talus slides (especially near the foot), near lumber mills (favoring those with ample discarded slabs near a moist, wooded periphery), and in other such habitats.

Size: Although these snakes may occasionally exceed 3½ feet (the record is 48¼ inches!), most found are very much smaller. A more normal length is 18–28 inches, and any specimen measuring more than 30 inches must be considered large indeed.

Identifying features: This beautiful tricolor has a triad count of 23–56. The snout is black but may be flecked with red. The banding is variable, with the red sometimes the narrowest and at other times the widest. The black and white bands are often of about equal width, but either may be the wider. The belly is primarily a patchy blackish gray and pale red, with the white bands often being broken ventrally. One pattern phase may predominate on one mountain chain and another pattern phase may predominate on the next mountain.

Similar species: None within the range.

PATTERN PHASES

56a. The phase formerly referred to as the St. Helena Mountain Kingsnake was described as *L. z. zonata*. It occurs in a small patch of wilderness north and a bit east of San Francisco Bay. The triad count is typically 24–30 (average of 27). The snout is black. The posterior edge of the first white band is posterior to the corner of the mouth. The black and white bands are of nearly equal width, and both of these colors are a bit narrower than the red.

California Mountain Kingsnake, St. Helena phase

California Mountain Kingsnake, Sierra phase

56b. The phase known as the Sierra Mountain Kingsnake (*L. z. multicincta*) takes its name from California's Sierra Nevada range. At high altitudes, where low nighttime temperatures restrict movement during much of the year, this kingsnake may be surface-active by day. Where temperatures are more moderate, it may indulge in crepuscular and nocturnal, as well as some diurnal, activity. This snake is noted for its variable coloration. Most specimens are clad in scales of red, black, and white. The red bands are usually precisely defined anteriorly, where they are at least twice as wide as either the black or the white bands. The black bands often narrow perceptibly posteriorly, but may widen and interrupt the red bands dorsally. The first white band is often comparatively narrow, and its rear edge is slightly posterior to the edge of the mouth. This snake has an average of 35 (23–48) triads (black-red-black). Some, or all, triads may lack red, so that part or all of the snake will be patterned just in black and white bands. This reduction of red seems more an individual than a populational trend. The belly color is paler than the dorsum, with the white bands being particularly irregular. It is in the central high Sierras that the snakes missing the red most often occur. This race normally has a black nose.

California Mountain Kingsnake, Coast phase

56c. The Coast Mountain Kingsnake pattern phase was formerly known as *L. z. multifasciata*. It tends to have narrow bands and a busy pattern. Typically the red bands are only marginally the widest. The white bands are next widest, and the black is the narrowest. The snout is black, but often has red patches or scales. With an average of 35, the triad count may vary from 26 to 45. The belly is paler and far more irregularly marked than the dorsum. The posterior edge of the first white band can be either behind or in front of the corner of the mouth. Rely primarily on range when attempting an identification of this snake. The coast mountain king-snake phase occurs in at least three disjunct areas in the coastal ranges, southward from the San Francisco Bay area to Orange County. Although it does occur in mountainous areas, it is not a rare snake in moist, shaded, rocky, sea-level canyons.

56d. The former San Bernardino Mountain Kingsnake (known for years as *L. z. parvirubra*) has a higher average triad count than the previous two races, with a low of 35 and a high of 56, and average triad count of 41. The red bands are noticeably, but not excessively, the widest, followed next in

California Mountain Kingsnake, San Bernardino phase

width by the white rings and then by the narrow black rings. Although all three colors are present on the belly, the markings there are pale and irregular. The posterior edge of the first white band either bisects or is at the anterior edge of the last upper labial scale. The snout tends to be entirely black in this pattern phase. Usually only a few of the red rings are broken dorsally by black pigment. This race also occurs at low elevations. It ranges in the foothills and wooded, stream-drained canyons of Los Angeles, San Bernardino, and Riverside counties in southern California.

56e. The southern California pattern phase was once called the San Diego Mountain Kingsnake and was identified by the scientific name of *L. z. pulchra*. It occurs in rock- and boulder-strewn habitats from sea level to foothills and isolated mountainsides in Los Angeles, Orange, Riverside, and San Diego counties. This snake has a black snout. The posterior edge of the first white band bisects the last upper labial, or may be slightly anterior to the anterior suture of that scale. Except for a reduced triad count, this phase is quite similar to the San Bernardino mountain kingsnake (account 56c). The triad count on the San Diego mountain kingsnake varies between 26 and 39, with an average of 33. The paler belly bears imprecisely delineated markings.

California Mountain Kingsnake, San Diego phase

Two additional subspecies occur in Mexico. These are *L. z. agalma*, the San Pedro Mountain Kingsnake, and the curious little black and white *L. z. herrarae*, the Todos Santos Island Kingsnake.

Gopher Snakes and Bullsnakes, Genus *Pituophis*

The members of this genus are moderately large to large snakes with heavily keeled scales, the ability to constrict, and a rather belligerent nature; because of a glottal modification they are able to hiss loudly, and they have a penchant for vibrating their tail. The head of the bull and gopher snakes is narrow, but moderately wider than the neck. The rostral scale—the scale on the tip of the snout—is protruding, strongly convex, and much higher than wide. There are four prefrontal scales. The body scales are in 27–35 (often 29) rows at midbody and the anal plate is undivided.

Depending on temperatures, these snakes are active either by day or by night.

A projecting supraocular scale makes the snakes of this genus appear as if they are scowling.

These snakes are accomplished burrowers, pursuing their rodent prey (some seem to be pocket gopher specialists) in their underground burrows as well as choosing underground chambers in areas of moist soil for egg deposition. All members of the genus are oviparous. Most clutches consist of relatively few (3–25) large eggs. Communal nesting is well documented in some species. As might be surmised, the hatchlings are also quite large, some exceeding 20 inches in length.

Despite having a very different appearance, the snakes of this genus are closely allied to the rat snakes and the kingsnakes. Captives of all three groups have been known to interbreed and produce fully viable young.

57. Pacific Gopher Snake

Pituophis catenifer catenifer

Abundance/Range: The range of this common snake includes much of western Oregon and California.

Habitat: From suburban fields to mountain fastnesses, from ranches and farmlands to remote canyons, from desert flats to irrigated fields and grasslands—these and more are the habitats of the Pacific gopher snake. They may be found at elevations of from sea level to close to 9,000 feet. Because of their fondness for burrowing mammals as prey, these snakes remain below the ground in the mammal burrows much of the time. In the confines of a gopher or rat burrow, where space renders it impossible to throw a constricting coil around the prey, the snakes press the rodent prey against the sides of the burrow, a particularly effective method of overpowering the toothy gophers. From one to several small mammals can be simultaneously overpowered either by this method or by typical constriction.

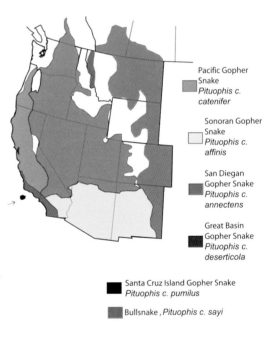

Pacific Gopher Snake *Pituophis c. catenifer*

Sonoran Gopher Snake *Pituophis c. affinis*

San Diegan Gopher Snake *Pituophis c. annectens*

Great Basin Gopher Snake *Pituophis c. deserticola*

Santa Cruz Island Gopher Snake *Pituophis c. pumilus*

Bullsnake, *Pituophis c. sayi*

Size: Although the Pacific gopher snake is one of the larger races, having been measured at up to 7 feet in total length, adults are more typically 4½–5 feet in length.

Pacific Gopher Snake, normal phase

Pacific Gopher Snake, striped phase

Identifying features: This is one of the more variable gopher snakes in both color and pattern. It occurs naturally in both blotched and striped morphs, and albino specimens of both are not particularly uncommon. The stripes can be variable in number and may not contrast sharply with the ground color. When present, the dorsal blotches are chocolate brown, usually discrete from each other and from the lateral spots, and well defined. The dorsal ground color is straw to straw gray, and the lateral ground color is strongly gray. Because of overlapping characteristics and intergradation, rely on range maps for subspecific assignment.

Similar species: The glossy snake and the various racers have smooth scales.

ADDITIONAL SUBSPECIES

58. The Sonoran Gopher Snake, *P. c. affinis*, is clad in earthen-colored scales and patterned in quiet camouflaging tones. Against a dorsal and lateral ground color of light brown, tan, or straw-yellow, it has anterior dorsal blotches of medium brown to almost russet. These do not contact the row of lateral spots. The dorsal blotches usually (but not always) darken to deep brown or black posteriorly and they may contact at least some of the lateral blotches, which are in 3 rows: a dorsolateral row that nestles between the dorsal blotches, a lateral row that is largest and alternates between the dorsolateral spots, and ventrolateral rows that are small, inconsistent, and on the outermost edges of every second or third ventral scute. The supracaudal spots are almost black. The belly is yellowish and

Sonoran Gopher Snake

has a variable number of bold, dark spots. The outer edges (sides) of the belly scutes are usually dusky. Hatchlings look very much like diminutive examples of the adults, but may be somewhat paler. Adults are 5–7 feet in length. The Sonoran gopher snake ranges southward from southern Colorado, through most of Arizona, New Mexico, and western Texas, to Sinaloa and northern Zacatecas, Mexico.

59. The San Diego Gopher Snake, *P. c. annectens*, occasionally exceeds 6 feet in length but is far more commonly seen in the range of 4–5 feet. The anterior dorsal blotches are quite dark (nearing black on some specimens) and may fuse both with each other and with the lateral blotches along each outer edge; this can produce a snake that is very dark in color. Many of the yellowish to tan ventral scutes have a dark spot (smudge) on their outermost extremes and may also have sparse spotting centrally. This race is found southward from Santa Barbara County, California, to central Baja California Norte. This snake seems most common in coastal areas, but it is also a well-known snake in both mountains and desert.

San Diego Gopher Snake

Great Basin Gopher Snake

60. The Great Basin Gopher Snake, *P. c. deserticola*, has been recorded at a length of 6 feet, but is typically well under 5 feet in length. This is a dark subspecies of gopher snakes that may have an imprecise pattern of interconnected blotches; however, some specimens have a light ground color and small, precise, and largely discrete dorsal and lateral blotches. The center of each light-colored dorsal scale bears a dark longitudinal line. The dorsal blotches of this inland race vary from almost black (or very deep brown) anteriorly to a pleasing dark to reddish brown posteriorly. The supracaudal markings are black and often interconnect with the lateral blotches, creating the illusion of a light-blotched dark snake rather than the opposite. Scale rows vary between 27 and 35. The range of the Great Basin gopher snake includes south central British Columbia (Canada) southward to southeastern California, northern Arizona, and extreme northwestern New Mexico.

61. The Santa Cruz Island Gopher Snake, *P. c. pumilus*, is a rather small snake (to about 3 feet) with a grayish ground color and a blotching that is a dusty black. The dorsal blotches are small and usually discrete. The upper sides are lightest, forming a dorsolateral stripe about 3 scales wide. The small dorsolateral spots are arranged along the top of this stripe, and

Santa Cruz Island Gopher Snake

the lateral spots along the ventral edge. The keeled scales are in 29 or fewer rows, and the anal plate is not divided. This seldom seen race occurs only on Santa Cruz, San Miguel, and Santa Rosa islands on the south side of California's Santa Barbara Channel.

62. The Bullsnake, *P. c. sayi*, is one of the most magnificent snakes of the American west. The strongly convex rostral scale of this snake is in the form of an acute triangle, and much higher than wide. Although most adult specimens seen are 3½–5½ feet in length, the record length is 8 feet 4 inches. Since this is a heavy-bodied snake that is apt to be defensive, finding one of more than 6 feet in length is a memorable occurrence. The ground color of the bullsnake varies from a pale straw yellow to a rather brilliant medium yellow (occasionally an evident, but pale, orange). The 40–66 dorsal blotches go from dark brown anteriorly, to lighter brown at midbody, to nearly black posteriorly. The 3 rows of lateral spots are colored similarly to the dorsal blotches. The dorsolateral spots, as well as those in the ventrolateral rows, are irregular and often poorly defined. There is a dark line from the eye to the corner of the mouth, and the upper and lower labial scales often have prominent, dark sutures. The venter is yellow with scattered dark spots and smudges, and there are spots on

Bullsnake

the outer edge (side) of every second ventral scute. Some specimens are dark and have poorly defined markings; others are prettily and precisely marked. The bullsnake occurs over a vast expanse of range. It may be found as far north as southern Alberta and southwestern Saskatchewan, Canada; as far south as southern Tamaulipas, Mexico; and from western Indian in the east, westward to western Montana. In central New Mexico and west Texas the bullsnake intergrades extensively with the Sonoran gopher snake.

Additional Mexican subspecies of *Pituophis catenifer* are known.

Long-nosed Snakes, Genus *Rhinocheilus*

Taxonomic note: Traditionally this genus has contained at least three mainland and one island subspecies. Two occurred in the United States and two in Mexico. Recent studies (2004), however, have determined that the characteristics used to differentiate the mainland subspecies are overlapping and not definitive. This has resulted in subspecific names being discontinued.

This is a secretive and capable burrower, but it may also be found amid sheltering rocks, in crevices, in rodent burrows, under debris, or otherwise hidden by day. The long-nosed snake often prowls widely in the evening and by night, especially during or following rains.

The long-nosed snake is considered a kingsnake relative. If provoked, it may either hide its head in its body coils, or assume an S and strike animatedly. Juveniles are especially apt to bite if molested. If severely stressed, long-nosed snakes autohemorrhage from the cloaca while voiding musk and feces. Nasal hemorrhaging has also been noted. The precise mechanics of this remain unknown, but it is thought to be restricted to females.

Long-nosed snakes are efficient constrictors, but often consume small prey items without constricting. While lizards seem the food of choice, small rodents and nestling birds are also eaten.

The head is slender; the nose is pointed. The smooth scales are in 23 rows and the anal plate is undivided. Many of the subcaudal scales are undivided also.

They are oviparous. One or rarely two clutches of 1–12 (usually 3–6) eggs are laid annually. Hatchlings average about 9 inches in length.

63. Long-nosed Snake

Rhinocheilus lecontei

Abundance/Range: This common snake ranges westward from extreme southwestern Kansas and southern Texas to southern Idaho, northern California, southern mainland Mexico, and the northern half of the Baja Peninsula.

Habitat: The long-nosed snake is a denizen of arid and semiarid lands. Look for it in rock- or boulder-strewn deserts, grasslands, and prairies. It is commonly seen crossing trans-desert roadways. It occurs primarily from sea level to altitudes of about 3,500 feet, but may rarely be encountered as high as 5,400 feet in elevation.

Size: Most examples of these slender snakes are 16–30 inches long. Specimens up to 42 inches in length have been recorded.

Identifying features: This is a pretty snake with a busy pattern. It may be either bicolored (black and white) or tricolored (black, white, and red).

Long-nosed Snake, tricolored phase

Long-nosed Snake, bicolored phase

The tricolored phase is the most common. The red scales, which are often restricted largely to the vertebral area, are tipped or flecked with yellow and narrowly edged with white. Yellow tipping (flecking), especially prevalent laterally, is also present on the black scales, and many of the yellow scales are flecked with black. The narrow head is primarily yellow with black flecks and sutures. The nose may be slightly upturned (eastern examples) or may not be upturned (western examples). The belly is yellow to cream and unpatterned except at the outer edges (sides) of some scutes. Some specimens lack all traces of red. On these, the whitish to yellowish ground color may not bear extensive flecking of black, but the black saddles are strongly flecked laterally with light pigment. The scales are smooth and in 23 rows, and the anal plate is nondivided. At least some of the subcaudal scales are not divided. Lizards figure very prominently in the diet of most specimens.

Similar snakes: Milk snakes and kingsnakes have all subcaudal scales divided. The coral snake has broad *rings* of black, red, and yellow, with the two caution colors (red and yellow) touching.

INSECT-EATING SONORINES

Sand Snakes, Genus *Chilomeniscus*

This species has a narrow head, smooth scales, and a concave venter. A favored habitat is the duff (decomposing vegetational litter) that surrounds desert plants growing in loose sand or gravelly habitats. Sand snakes can be found in desert habitats as variable as those supporting mesquite-creosote bush or thornscrub associations or in areas of open dunes. It moves with remarkable speed and dexterity through yielding surface sands, leaving an indented trail behind as the sand collapses into the snake's tunnel.

The sand snake eats a variety of burrowing arthropods, including many insects and their pupae. They seem especially fond of tenebrionid beetle larvae and roaches. Centipedes are also occasionally eaten.

Between 2 and 4 eggs have been documented in a clutch. Hatchlings are a bit under 4 inches in length.

Scales are in 13 rows; the anal plate is divided.

64. Variable Sand Snake

Chilomeniscus stramineus

Taxonomic note: This snake was formerly known as the banded sand snake, *C. cinctus*. Although those in the United States are all of the banded phase, a broad range of colors is found in Mexico. Among other colors, Mexican sand snakes may be brightly banded in pink, red, or yellow and black, banded in grays and tans, have black dots on the scales, or be uniform sandy brown. It has been found that rather than being several species as was originally thought, these variations are all phases

Variable Sand Snake

of the same species. The common name was changed to reflect this variability and *C. stramineus* became the scientific name.

Abundance/Range: Variable sand snakes are fairly common but, because of their fossorial proclivities, not often seen. When they do surface, it is usually after nightfall or during heavy rains. This species ranges southward from central and western Arizona to both Sonora on mainland Mexico and the Baja Peninsula.

Size: This is one of the smallest snakes of the southwestern United States. It is adult at 6½–11 inches in length. It is of fair girth.

Habitat: A desert snake, the variable sand snake utilizes a specialized burrowing method termed sand-swimming. In keeping with this, it is a creature that should be looked for in areas of fine to coarse yielding sand, often in the vicinity of plant communities of mesquite, creosote bush, saguaro, and ocotillo.

Identifying features: In the United States this is a beautiful little candycane snake. The ground color is cream to yellow, often brighter, or even shading to strawberry, dorsally, and the black saddles, which reach well down onto the sides of the body, actually encircle the short, stout, tail. The dark saddles may be narrow and numerous or broad and few. The head is narrow, the snout is flattened, the lower jaw is prominently countersunk, the nostrils are valvular, and the eyes are small but fully functional. The nose is light in color and weakly convex. The concave belly is off-white to pale yellow. The scales are smooth. The rather large rostral scale curves back over the snout, separating the internasal scales.

Similar species: The internasal scales of both species of shovel-nosed snakes are not separated by the rostral scale. Banded examples of the ground snake lack the prominently countersunk lower jaw, and the scales are usually in 15 rows, at least anteriorly. The Arizona coral snake has 15 rows of scales and is distinctively patterned in broad rings of black, red, and yellow. The caution colors, red and yellow, touch.

ADDITIONAL SUBSPECIES

None.

Shovel-nosed Snakes, Genus *Chionactis*

This is a genus of two species of burrowing, sand-swimming desert snakes that, like the variable sand snake, have a narrow head, a concave belly, and nonkeeled scales. The rostral scale (the scale on the tip of the snout) is large, cornified, and spadelike. The tail is not foreshortened as it is on the variable sand snake.

These two species of small desert snakes feed exclusively on invertebrate prey. Insects, spiders, centipedes, and small scorpions are all eaten. The larvae and pupae of tenebrionid beetles are relished. Much of the food is found during the snake's burrowing activities.

Comparatively little is known about the reproductive biology of the shovel-nosed snakes. They are oviparous and lay 2–5 eggs (occasionally more) in each clutch. Egg deposition occurs in the late spring to early summer. Hatchlings are about 4 inches long.

These snakes are slender and supple, often strike animatedly when startled, and are usually seen above ground only after nightfall. They move quickly when disturbed. They can be abundant in prime, loose-sand habitats. If on a smooth roadway, they may slide about in their efforts to move quickly.

These interesting little desert snakes are often present in numbers much greater than thought. Should you choose to see one, slowly drive a paved desert road after dark and watch for the fast moving snakes in the glow of the headlights. Unless you are absolutely certain what species it is you are seeing, it is best to just look and don't touch.

65. Mojave Shovel-nosed Snake

Chionactis occipitalis occipitalis

Abundance/Range: Because of its fossorial habits, even where it is an abundant species, the Mojave shovel-nosed snake is much more often seen as it crosses roadways than in natural habitat. It does often crawl on the surface in the early evening, or during and following rain storms. This snake is found from central Arizona and southern Nevada to central southern California.

☐ Mojave Shovel-nosed Snake, *Chionactis o. occipitalis*

▨ Colorado Desert Shovel-nosed Snake, *Chionactis o. annulata*

▨ Tucson Shovel-nosed Snake, *Chionactis o. klauberi*

▨ Nevada Shovel-nosed Snake, *Chionactis o. talpina*

Habitat: The Mojave shovel-nose is a fossorial desert snake that swims rapidly through loose-sand habitats. It is most frequently seen in areas of fine sand, but may also be encountered in coarser sand habitats. It has been found both where vegetation is sparse, and where vegetation is relatively thick. The mounds of yielding sands associated with the root systems of desert shrubs and kangaroo rat middens are excellent microhabitats.

Size: This snake is adult at 11–14 inches in total length. Occasional specimens of 16–17 inches in length have been authenticated.

Identifying features: This is a brown and yellow, or brown yellow, and pale red banded snake. There are more than 24 dark bands. Most do not span the belly. The nose is light in color. The rostral scale is broad and shovel-like, and the forehead is rather flat. The tail is not noticeably shortened. The shiny scales lack a keel and are usually in 15 rows. The anal plate is divided. The two internasals are in contact on the top of the snout. The sloping snout is flat in profile. The belly is concave, an adaptation to help the snake gain purchase as it swims through the loose sand. The lower jaw is noticeably countersunk and the nostrils are valvular.

Similar species: The Arizona coral snake is brightly ringed in red, black, and yellow and has a black nose. The banded sand snake is shorter and

Mojave Desert Shovel-nosed Snake

stouter. It has a very short tail and scales in 13 rows, and the internasals are separated by the rostral scale. The nose of the ground snake is not specialized for burrowing, and there is usually some dark shading on each light scale. The Organ Pipe shovel-nosed snake is more strongly crossbanded, has brighter colors and usually 20 or fewer black crossbands.

ADDITIONAL SUBSPECIES

An additional three races of shovel-nosed snakes have been described. Where ranges abut, specimens with overlapping or confusing characteristics may be found. The easternmost and southernmost races tend to be most brightly and contrastingly colored.

66. The Colorado Desert Shovel-nosed Snake, *C. o. annulata*, ranges westward from central and western Arizona to southeastern California and southward to northern Mexico. The ground color of this subspecies is of some shade of pale yellow to cream. There are usually 25 or fewer well-separated, rather narrow, dark (usually black) bands, many of which completely encircle the body (cross the belly). In each wide yellow band there is usually a narrow, partial band of pale red. A broad, dark marking in the form of an open U curves backward from each eye over the top of the head. The first neck band is broad and does not encircle the body. The

nose is light in color. The rostral scale is broad and shovel-like, and the forehead is rather flat.

Colorado Desert Shovel-nosed Snake, tricolored phase

Colorado Desert Shovel-nosed Snake, bicolored phase

67. The Tucson Shovel-nosed Snake, *C. o. klauberi*, is the easternmost of the races. It is found primarily in Pinal and Pima counties Arizona. The black primary bands of this shovel-nosed snake are quite wide dorsally, narrow dramatically on the sides, but often continue across the belly. More poorly defined secondary bands of black are usually present. The red, although fairly bright, is often reduced to small dorsal blotches. This subspecies seems to be becoming increasingly rare, especially in the southernmost portion of its range.

Tucson Shovel-nosed Snake

68. The Nevada Shovel-nosed Snake, *C. o. talpina*, is the northernmost representative of this species. It ranges westward to eastern central California from southwestern Nevada. It is the palest race, having brown rather than black primary crossbands, a hint of brownish secondary bands in the light fields, and a creamy ground color. Many bands do not continue across the belly. Some red may be present in the light areas. There are many (152 or more) ventral scales.

Nevada Shovel-nosed Snake

69. Organ Pipe Shovel-nosed Snake
Chionactis palarostris organica

Abundance/Range: Actual population statistics are sparse. This is an uncommonly encountered snake species in the United States. It is seen with somewhat more frequency in Mexico. In the United States, this species is known only from, and immediately north of, Organ Pipe Cactus National Monument, Pima County, Arizona. The range extends southward into Sonora, Mexico.

Habitat: This snake is associated with gravelly and rocky flats in areas vegetated by saguaro, ocotillo, creosote bush, and associated shrubs.

Size: The Organ Pipe shovel-nose is a tiny burrowing snake. It is adult at 10–12 inches in total length. The largest documented size is 15½ inches.

Identifying features: This is a smooth-scaled, shiny, diminutive, and beautiful snake. The red markings are saddles, not rings, and rather narrowly edged with the yellowish ground color. There are about 20 black rings, which narrow ventrally. The snout, and most of the belly, is yellowish. The snout is weakly convex. The lower jaw is countersunk. The scales are in 15 rows, and the anal plate is divided.

Organ Pipe Shovel-nosed Snake

Similar species: The Arizona coral snake has a black nose and clear, wide rings of black, red, and yellow (the red and yellow caution colors touch). Other species of shovel-nosed snakes in the Organ Pipe Cactus National Monument region have a flat (not convex) snout, and they usually have more than 20 black rings, and fewer well-defined red saddles. Banded specimens of the ground snake do not have prominently countersunk lower jaws and usually lack most yellow dorsally. The long-nosed snake is much larger when adult and has black flecks in the red and yellow fields and yellow flecks in the black.

A Trio of Arizonans

Southeastern and south central Arizona are the northernmost strongholds for several Mexican reptile and amphibian species. Of these, three in particular have long intrigued me. These are the little tricolored thornscrub hook-nosed snake, *Gyalopion quadrangulare*, the attenuate and inordinately slender brown vine snake, *Oxybelis aeneus*, and the very beautiful Organ Pipe shovel-nosed snake, *Chionactis palarostris organica*.

I have made many excursions to the Arizona ranges of these species, but have not yet found either the hook-nose or the vine snake north of the border.

That all three occur in fair numbers seems certain, for several of each are found each summer. In fact, some researchers have found more than one of each on a single trip.

The hook-nose is a tiny, heavy-bodied terrestrial species that feeds on insects, centipedes, and scorpions. Rather common in northwestern Mexico, it is considered an uncommon snake in the United States, where it occurs only in the vicinity of Ruby, Arizona. Time after time I have made the grueling run from my east coast home to southern Arizona only to fail. And this has been the case with the arboreal brown vine snake as well. With friends and alone I have walked the lonely canyons along the Mexican border, finding rare frogs, uncommon turtles, and beautiful insects, but never a vine snake. Well, next year I'll try again.

But I can now cross the Organ Pipe shovel-nose off of my "need to see" list, for in 2003, while motoring northward from the Mexican border, we found one of these beautiful, red orange, black and white, insectivorous

continued

burrowers just north of Organ Pipe National Monument. It was Kenny Wray, half asleep in the shotgun seat, who spotted the little snake as it was darting across the roadway and screamed, "Stop!" It took a while, but we were lucky. The snake was still on the road after we skidded to a stop. It was with joy and wonderment that we both took picture after picture of the coveted snake, a species for which we had both searched for more than a decade.

Western Hook-nosed Snakes, Genus *Gyalopion*

The genus *Gyalopion* is represented in the western United States by two species. Of these, one, *G. canum*, the Chihuahuan hook-nosed snake, occurs from central Texas to eastern Arizona, and *G. quadrangulare*, the thornscrub hook-nosed snake, pushes northward from its Mexican stronghold only into extreme south central Arizona. These snakes are associated with thornscrub and creosote bush at lower elevations, but also occur at elevations of up to 1 mile. Although secretive burrowers, both species often prowl the desert surface after nightfall, and may be found crossing roadways well into the wee hours of the morning.

Both feed on invertebrate prey items. Spiders and beetle larvae are reportedly the prey of choice, but they also consume other invertebrates such as scorpions and centipedes.

These snakes have grooved, slightly enlarged teeth at the rear of the upper jaw and a proteinaceous saliva. It is speculated that the saliva may benumb the snake's invertebrate prey. Both species are harmless to humans and, although they will strike at a prodding finger, they can seldom be induced to bite. When prodded, this species writhes animatedly and pops its cloacal lining in and out, producing a snapping sound—a defense mechanism of unknown value.

Because of their strongly upturned rostral scale, these snakes look superficially like diminutive hog-nosed snakes. They are proportionately stout, with short, stout tails that taper quickly to a point. Both species have smooth scales in 17 rows. *G. canum* has a divided anal plate while that of *G. quadrangulare* is undivided.

Little is known about the reproductive biology of either species. Female *G. canum* are known to contain 1–4 full-term eggs. Two eggs were found in a road-killed female *G. quadrangulare*. Hatchling size of either species is unknown.

70. Chihuahuan Hook-nosed Snake

Gyalopion canum

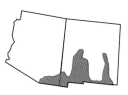

Abundance/Range: Western hook-nosed snakes are fairly common, but because of their fossorial proclivities and nocturnal habits, they are not often seen. Heavy summer rains may induce them to surface in fair numbers. The range of this species in the United States extends westward through southern New Mexico to southeastern Arizona from central Texas. It also occurs in northern interior Mexico.

Size: This tiny snake is adult at 6½–9½ inches in length. The largest recorded adult was just over 15 inches long.

Identifying features: The ground color of the western hook-nosed snake is tan, cinnamon, or gray(ish). There are from 25 to more than 40 dark brown dorsal bands. All bands may be similar in intensity, or there may be primary bands and secondary bands. The bands are usually best defined dorsally, where they are bordered both anteriorly and posteriorly by a narrow dark edging. If present as a series of alternating primary and secondary bands, the latter may be present on only one side, be present on

Chihuahuan Hook-nosed Snake

both sides but broken dorsally, or be virtually entire. The lowermost two rows of lateral scales are white except where patterned by the dark dorsal bands. The head is only slightly wider than the neck. The eyes are small but fully functional and have round pupils. A dark subocular blotch and a wide, dark, interorbital bar are both present. A second dark marking is present on the back of the head as either a complete bar or as a dark spot on each side. The venter is white to off-white.

Similar species: Rather than being free edged and sharpened anteriorly, the rostral of both species of leaf-nosed snakes curves back up over the snout. The rostral scale of the western hog-nosed snake is strongly keeled above. The top of the head of the extralimital Mexican hook- nosed snake, *Ficimia streckeri,* lacks dark bars. The thornscrub hook-nosed snake has rose red sides.

71. Thornscrub Hook-nosed Snake

Gyalopion quadrangulare

Abundance/Range: Little is known about the actual population statistics of this snake in Arizona, but the thornscrub is the least frequently seen of the three species of hook-nosed snakes in the United States. Since in Arizona it is at the periphery of its range, this is not entirely unexpected. It is much more frequently seen (but, perhaps, no better understood) in Mexico. This snake ranges northward to south-eastern Arizona. There it is best known from Santa Cruz County, but may also occur in Pima and Cochise counties. Its exact range in the United States remains badly in need of defining. In Mexico this species ranges southward along the Pacific Coast to the state of Nyarit.

Habitat: As indicated by its common name, this snake is associated with thornscrub and creosote bush desert at lower elevations, but also occurs to altitudes of more than 4,000 feet in the Patagonia and Pajarito mountains. It is known to be a burrower in habitats varying from canyon bottoms to open grasslands. It is induced to the surface by summer rains and has been found on rare occasions crossing roadways after nightfall.

Size: This seldom seen species is adult at 5–9½ inches in length. Large adults may approach a foot in length.

Thornscrub Hook-nosed Snake

Identifying features: This is the brightest colored and most spectacularly marked of the hook-nosed snakes. The 30–36 black saddles are broadest and best defined dorsally and tend to be wider anteriorly than posteriorly. The downward projecting lateral extensions are infiltrated interstitially by light gray. The dorsal ground color, between the dark saddles, is a pale grayish white. A rust red to rose red lateral stripe is present on the upper sides, 2½–5 scales wide. This may be partially broken by the black of the lateral projections of the dorsal markings. Below the red stripe the lateral color is again grayish white. The belly is a uniform white, often with a greenish overlay. A dark interorbital extends rearward and is contiguous with a broad nuchal blotch. The cheeks are rust red. The eyes are small, have round pupils, and are fully functional. The projecting rostral scale is sharp edged and upturned, but is not keeled dorsally, and, posteriorly, separates the internasal scales.

Similar snakes: The enlarged rostral scale of both species of leaf-nosed snakes curves back up over the snout. The rostral scale of the western hog-nosed snake is strongly keeled above, and the body scales are also keeled. The western hook-nosed snake lacks distinctive rosy red flanks and has narrow dorsal blotches.

Ground Snakes, Genus *Sonora*

There are few snakes in America as variably colored as these snakes. Depending on the simplicity or complexity of the pattern and colors, it may be easy or difficult to mistake a ground snake for other small snake species. In general, it might be said that ground snakes lack any distinctly overt physical identifying characteristics. They are a very typical small snake species. The head is only moderately distinct from the neck. The scales are in 13–15 rows and are smooth. The anal plate is divided. A loreal scale (usually distinct, sometimes partially fused to another scale) broadly separates the second upper labial from the prefrontal scale on each side. This is an important identifying characteristic.

Ground snakes are usually associated with well-drained plains, prairies, semideserts, and desert-edge habitats. These secretive little snakes may be found in numbers in areas where flat surface rocks are abundant. They are secretive but may become surface active in force on warm, damp, spring nights.

Sonora feed upon small arthropods, and occasionally on tiny geckos and their eggs. They have a weakly toxic saliva and prey on arachnids, including such noxious types as small scorpions and centipedes. Crickets and other insects, larvae, and spiders are also accepted. The toxic saliva aids in overpowering insects and perhaps as a predigestant. One researcher has reported finding a *Sonora* attempting to swallow a road-killed Texas banded gecko. It is not known whether these nocturnal lizards figure prominently in the diet of the ground snake.

This is an oviparous species. Up to 6 eggs may be laid in a clutch. Incubation duration is about 60 days. Hatchlings measure 4–5 inches in length.

72. Variable Ground Snake

Sonora semiannulata semiannulata

Abundance/Range: This snake is often the predominant species within a given area; yet it is usually seldom seen. When the ground snake does surface it is usually after nightfall or during heavy rains. This species ranges southward from central and eastern Kansas to Zacatecas, Mexico, then westward to the Baja Peninsula, eastern California, and northwestern Nevada. Disjunct populations occur as far northward as southwestern Idaho, Utah, southeastern Colorado, and north central Kansas.

Habitat: A desert, semidesert, grassland, ranchland species, the ground snake is primarily associated with open, rocky areas. It is commonly found beneath natural debris such as rocks and human-generated surface debris. It is often found near stock tanks, in the beds of intermittent streams and rivers, and in nearly any other habitat that offers ample cover and some amount of moisture.

Size: This small snake is adult at 8–12 (very rarely to 18) inches in total length, and is rather stocky.

Identifying features: The ground snake is one of the most variable of American snakes, both in coloration and in pattern. Among other

color and pattern schemes, these little terrestrial snakes may be unicolor russet, buff, or gray (sometimes with a vaguely darker head); may be distinctly banded in two tones of gray; may be greenish buff or gray with a prominent terra-cotta vertebral stripe (which may, or may not, be broken by broad black saddles); banded russet and buff; banded gray and pink (or red); be pinkish or russet dorsally, with black saddles and yellowish sides;

Variable Ground Snake

Variable Ground Snake

Variable Ground Snake

or be of a single ground color but have a dark spot on each light scale. The head is relatively narrow, but is slightly wider than the neck. A loreal scale is present. The lower jaw is not significantly countersunk.

Similar snakes: Because of the myriad color combinations and patterns exhibited by the ground snake, it can be mistaken for many other species. None of the black-headed snakes have any banding or contrastingly colored middorsal stripe, and all lack a loreal scale. Blind snakes have no functional eyes. Banded sand snakes and shovel-nosed snakes have a noticeably inset lower jaw and flattened snouts.

Black-headed Snakes, Genus *Tantilla*

In the American west the members of this genus are small, slender burrowers. Most are characterized by a black crown and, sometimes, a black nape. The head color may or may not be separated from the neck color by a light band.

The unicolored dorsum is often the color of the substrate on which these snakes are found. There is no loreal scale, an important fact when trying to separate these snakes from certain colorations of the ground snake. They are even more difficult to separate from each other. Hemipenial structure is often used by taxonomists to help identify a snake in hand. If it is necessary to resort to this latter, it is obviously only the males that can be identified. Rely strongly on range to facilitate identification.

The black-headed snakes are creatures of sandy, well-drained areas. They may occasionally be found beneath flat stones and building debris, and, even more occasionally, they may be surface active. Despite their persistent secrecy, these snakes vary by species from common and fairly well known, to rare and poorly understood.

The scales of these snakes are in 15 rows; the anal plate is divided.

Although possessing a toxic saliva and grooved rear teeth, the crowned snakes are reluctant to bite and are considered harmless to humans.

All prey on insects and other arthropods. Many seem to prefer centipedes, immobilized by the toxins in the saliva.

All species are oviparous and lay 1–4 (usually 1) eggs per clutch. It is thought that some females may double clutch. Deposition occurs during early summer. Hatchlings of the various western species vary by species from 3½ to about 4½ inches in length.

Black-headed Snakes: An Elusive Californian

"It's a black-headed snake," said Regis.

And indeed it was.

Regis Opferman had flipped a piece of cardboard on the sandy right-of-way just to the southeast of Pueblo, Colorado, and beneath it had been a worm-sized Southwestern black-headed snake. Regis was happy, for it was a lifer for him. I was happy, for I now had a chance to photograph a species that I had worked very hard to find.

Even harder for me has been the California black-headed snake (as in, I have failed to find it). Although I have seen several on the roads of San Diego County, California, all have been traffic fatalities. In fact, had it not been for the generosity of Anish Yelekar, I would not yet have a living example to photograph.

And that's the way it often is. There are times when even common snakes evade our every effort to find them, all the while being readily found by colleagues driving the same roads that we have driven or turning the same surface debris that we have turned.

Field observation is about 40 percent skill and 60 percent luck, and I try never to forget that.

73. Smith's Black-headed Snake
Tantilla hobartsmithi

Taxonomic Comments: This species used to be called the southwestern black-headed snake.

Abundance/Range: Although very seldom seen, this little snake is not thought to be rare. On the very rare occasions when it does surface, it is usually after nightfall or when to the surface by flooding or heavy rains.

Smith's black-headed snake has a discontinuous range, occurring in several disjunct colonies in southern, central, and western Arizona, southern Utah, extreme central-western Colorado, southern New Mexico and western Texas, southern California, and northern Mexico.

Habitat: A desert and grassland snake, Smith's black-headed snake occurs in areas as diverse as those that host growths of yucca, mesquite, and creosote bush, as well as in juniper scrublands and open conifer-

ous woodlands. However, it seems most common at low elevations in limestone habitats near springs or other sources of moisture. This snake is persistently fossorial, burrowing readily through yielding soils, as well are whitish, sometimes with an opalescent cast. The dark cap is largely restricted to the top of the head and seldom goes lower on the sides of the head than the bottom of the eye. It extends rearward approximately 2 or 3 scale rows past the parietal shields. There may be (but often is not) a vaguely defined, narrow, light collar separating the dark head color from the gray body color. There is no loreal scale (see diagram of snake head, page 2). The scales are in 15 rows and the anal plate is divided.

Similar snakes: Rely primarily on range to identify this snake. Except in southeastern Arizona, where it and three other species occur, the range of this species is not known to overlap with the range of any other black-headed snake. Also see accounts 74–77, the Plains, western, Chihuahuan, and Yaqui black-headed snakes, respectively.

ADDITIONAL SUBSPECIES

None.

Smith's Black-headed Snake

74. Plains Black-headed Snake

Tantilla nigriceps

Abundance/Range: This is a seldom seen, but not uncommon snake species. It ranges eastward and southward from north central Colorado to western Kansas and northern Mexico.

Habitat: Grassy plains, desert grasslands, moist, rocky hillsides, and similar habitats are colonized by this snake. It is seldom seen above ground, but is often found beneath natural cover such as rocks and fallen plants and human-generated surface debris. It seems most common in sandy, yielding soils.

Size: This is another relatively small black-headed snake. It is adult at 7–10 inches in length, and the largest recorded specimen was a slender 14¾ inches.

Identifying features: This little snake has an olive gray to yellowish gray dorsum, and a pinkish to orange midventral area. On either side of this strip of color the venter is white. The dark cap extends from 2 to 5 scales

Plains Black-headed Snake

posterior to the parietal shields and tends to be pointed rather than smoothly rounded. The dark cap color usually extends downward only to the top of the upper labial scales. A light collar is usually absent.

Similar species: Check accounts 73, 75, 76, 77 for descriptions of other black-headed snakes.

ADDITIONAL SUBSPECIES

None.

75. Western Black-headed Snake

Tantilla planiceps

Abundance/Range: Like other members of this genus, the western black-headed snake is seldom seen, but is quite common in suitable habitat. This snake occurs in several disjunct ranges in coastal California from the vicinity of San Francisco Bay southward to the international boundary, and from there south to mid-Baja California.

Habitat: This secretive snake is a persistent burrower that occurs in habitats as diverse as grasslands, open hardwood areas, and semi-deserts. It is most often found beneath rocks, logs, and human-generated debris.

Western Black-headed Snake

Size: Although this slender snake has a recorded maximum length of 15½ inches, examples of more than 9 inches in length are rarely seen.

Identifying features: The dorsum is colored in earthen hues of from olive brown to yellowish brown. The venter is white, except for a pinkish to orangish central strip. The western black-headed snake has a very dark and extensive cap. The black cap extends from 2 to 3 scale rows posterior to the parietal scales, is vaguely rounded or straight on its posterior edge, and usually drops well below the mouthline posterior to the corner of the jaw. There is usually a moderately defined to well-defined narrow light collar posterior to the black of the head. The collar may be edged posteriorly by half-dark scales.

Similar species: While the range of no other black-headed snake overlaps that of this species, the range of Smith's black-headed snake (account 73) does lie near it. The silvery legless lizard, *Anniella pulchra*, lacks a black cap and has eyelids.

ADDITIONAL SUBSPECIES

None.

76. Chihuahuan Black-headed Snake

Tantilla wilcoxi wilcoxi

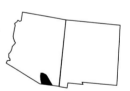

Abundance/Range: The Chihuahuan black-headed snake is thought to be uncommon in its limited Arizona range. This Mexican snake enters the United States only in the vicinity of the Huachuca Mountains in southeastern Arizona. It is not particularly uncommon south of our border.

Habitat: A secretive and fossorial species, the Chihuahuan black-headed snake may occasionally be found beneath plant debris, surface rocks, and human-generated debris. It occasionally actively crawls on the surface of the ground at night in warm, preferably damp, weather.

Size: The record size for this species is 14 inches. Specimens between 7 and 10 inches are more commonly seen.

Identifying features: The dorsal color is brown to olive brown. Some lateral scales contain a dark spot. The venter is white anteriorly and shades

Chihuahuan Black-headed Snake. Photo by Wayne Van Devender

to orange posteriorly. The black cap is of reduced length on this species, not including the rear tips of the parietal scales. Of the four species of black-headed snakes that occur in southeastern Arizona, this is the only one that has the posterior tips of the parietal scales included in the white collar. The white collar also includes at least one subsequent scale row. It is bordered posteriorly with dark scales. Most upper labials are light, but the black cap tips downward at the rear of the mouth, includes the rear half of the last supralabial scale, and touches (or may extend below) the jawline.
Similar species: See descriptions of other black-headed snakes (accounts 73, 74, 75, and 77).
Comments: This is one of the most infrequently seen snakes in our area. This species is occasionally referred to as the Huachuca black-headed snake.

ADDITIONAL SUBSPECIES

None in the United States.

77. Yaqui Black-headed Snake

Tantilla yaquia

Abundance/Range: Apparently uncommon in its limited United States range, the Yaqui black-headed snake is another Mexican species that barely enters the United States, where it is known to occur only in southeastern Arizona and immediately adjacent New Mexico.

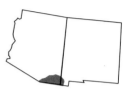

Habitat: In the United States, this uncommon snake occurs in loose soils in evergreen and deciduous woodlands. Many specimens have been found in riparian situations. In Mexico it also occurs on the coastal plain. As secretive as any other member of this genus, the Yaqui black-headed snake has been found beneath rocks, fallen vegetation, and human-generated debris.

Size: This is the smallest of the five species of black-headed snake in the American west. The Yaqui black-headed snake attains an adult size of only 13 inches, and those most frequently seen are 6–9 inches in length.

Identifying features: The Yaqui black-headed snake has a dorsum of light brown to olive brown or tan. The black cap extends for up to 4 scale rows posterior to the interparietal suture. The cap is widest anteriorly, extending under the eye and including all but the upper labial scales. The cap narrows posterior to the eye, forms a prominent cheek patch, then widens again, tipping downward to or past the corner of the mouth. No other

Yaqui Black-headed Snake

black-headed snake in the American west has a white cheek patch. The collar is variably distinct, but is usually broad and at least partially edged by dark scales posteriorly. The belly is orangish posteriorly and cream colored anteriorly. The smooth scales are in 15 rows and the anal plate is divided.

Similar snakes: See also accounts 73–76 for descriptions of other black-headed snakes.

SUBFAMILY DIPSADINAE: SHARP-TAILED SNAKES, RING-NECKED SNAKES, AND FANGLESS NIGHT SNAKES

Primarily a tropical family, in the American and Canadian west this family contains only three genera of small, secretive, often burrowing snakes. All have long teeth and toxic components in the saliva. None are harmful to man and most cannot be induced to bite.

Sharp-tailed Snake, Genus *Contia*

This genus occurs only from northern California northward to southern British Columbia. The single described species is fossorial and is active at temperatures as low as 50°F—temperatures when many (if not most) other snakes would be inactive. The sharp-tailed snake is a slug-eating specialist and has proportionately long teeth to enable it to hold such slippery prey.

The components of the saliva of this little snake are relatively unstudied, but it virtually never bites and, even if it should, it would be of no medical consequence to humans.

In many respects, the sharp-tailed snake is the ecological equivalent of the diminutive worm snakes of eastern United States. Both of these snakes have a tailtip scale that has modified into a sharp spine. Although totally harmless, the spine, when pushed against a captor, is sometimes so startling that the snake is dropped.

Very little is known about the reproductive biology of the sharp-tailed snake. It is an oviparous snake species. Females lay 2–8 (normal clutch size is 3–5) eggs in late summer. The incubation period is unknown, but is thought to be about 60 days, with the hatchlings emerging in mid-autumn.

Small Serpents of the Night

Snakes of the genus *Hypsiglena* are abundant denizens of our aridlands, from Texas to the Pacific Coast and from southern British Columbia to deep into Mexico.

In some parts of our arid southwest, night snakes are backyard species drawn to the edges of irrigated gardens and other sources of water. But they are also found in desert habitats and may be very common amid boulder fields or wherever else ground cover is plentiful.

Night snakes are often the first species you see crossing roads in the evening and may very well be the last species you see at night.

Depending on which authority you follow, there may be no subspecies or there may be five or even more.

One thing seems certain—no matter where you are within the range of this widespread western snake, they are variably colored, and, except for the constant dark nuchal blotches, the pattern may be variable also.

Reptile enthusiasts often seek snakes by "road-hunting"—driving back and forth on likely looking stretches of road (sometimes 100 or more miles long) from dusk until far into the night. On a good night, a night when reptiles and amphibians are active, this can be an enjoyable challenge for hobbyist or researcher, finding, identifying, and cataloging the species seen. But on a quiet night the tedium of the drive may be broken by finding only one or two reptiles, and as often as not these will be night snakes.

As a field herper and photographer, I have experienced both kinds of night.

There have been nights when, as I drove the long stretch of roadway through Anza Borrego State Park, there were so many sidewinders, shovel-nosed, leaf-nosed, and glossy snakes crossing, that it was almost impossible to keep the tally. But there have been many nights of the other kind as well, those nights when I would leave the motel a few minutes before dusk and not return until false dawn was staining the eastern horizon, and have only one snake on the tally sheet—and almost invariably this would be a night snake. Thank heavens they're out there to break the monotony of a bad night.

78. Sharp-tailed Snake

Contia tenuis

Abundance/Range: *Contia tenuis* is so secretive that census statistics are virtually impossible. It is probably not rare in suitable habitats, but it is rather seldom seen. Sharp-tailed snakes are found along both sides of Sacramento Valley in northern California, northward to northwestern Oregon (excluding the coastline), and in several disjunct colonies in the state of Washington, Vancouver Island, and South and North Pinder Island, British Columbia.

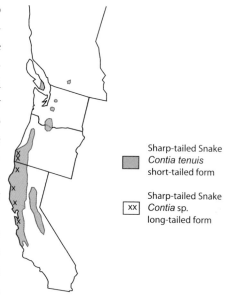

Sharp-tailed Snake
Contia tenuis
short-tailed form

Sharp-tailed Snake
xx *Contia sp.*
long-tailed form

Habitat: Although it is often found in very dry microhabitats (such as in cairns of gravel or pebbles), soil moisture is mandatory for the survival of this snake. It occurs from sea level stream edges to foggy mountaintop meadows up to 6,600 feet. It is an accomplished burrower into damp substrates, and may also be found behind the loosened bark of dead and decomposing trees (both fallen and standing), under

Sharp-tailed Snake

rocks, and beneath moisture-retaining, human-generated debris. The sharp-tailed snake is occasionally surface active, especially during or following rains.

Size: Although a maximum length of 18 inches has been documented for this snake, such a size is almost never seen. Most found are between 8 and 12 inches in length. Hatchlings are about 3 inches long.

Identifying features: This is a variably colored snake. Its dorsal coloration may be gray, earthen red, or russet, but its sides are grayish. The dorsal coloration is often a little brighter posteriorly. Dorsal and lateral colors are often delineated and separated by a reddish dorsolateral stripe on each side. The head is only slightly wider than the neck. The belly is white with a crossbar of black across the anterior edge of each of the ventral plates from chin to vent. Black pigment sometimes occurs on the outermost edges of the subcaudal scales. The smooth dorsal scales are in 15 rows at midbody. The anal plate is divided. The terminal tail scale is modified into a spine. The pupil is round. Hatchlings are reddish and have narrow dark lines on their sides that are sometimes retained in faded version into adulthood.

Similar species: The black and white barred venter and the tailtip spine are diagnostic and are shared with no other snake species in our region.

78a. The existence of a "long-tailed" morph of the short-tailed snake is now well known but the snake has not yet been scientifically described.

Forest Sharp-tailed Snake

The researchers have tentatively called this creature the Forest Short-tailed Snake. It has been differentiated from the more common morph by comparative tail length and subcaudaul scale count, ventral scute count, and preferred habitat. It is thought to be restricted to forested habitats and is known to be active at temperatures in the low 50s°F.

ADDITIONAL SUBSPECIES

None at this time.

Ring-necked Snakes, Genus *Diadophis*

There is only a single species of ring-necked snake, but by most standard accounts there are eight subspecies indigenous to the western United States. However, the characteristics initially used to differentiate these races overlap widely and are often not definitive. This has led some researchers to identify the snake only to species. Additional clarification of the geographic variation is needed.

With but two exceptions in the United States, the members of this group are easily identified to genus by their brilliant orange to orange red neck rings. The two that may have the rings muted or lacking are the Key ring-necked snake, *Diadophis punctatus acricus*, of Florida's Big Pine Key, and the regal ring-necked snake, *D. p. regalis*, of the western plains states and the southwest.

Ring-necks have varied dietary preferences and a toxic saliva to help them overcome their chosen prey. Their diet consists of (but is not necessarily limited to) slugs, earthworms, salamanders, tiny ground-dwelling lizards (such as hatchling skinks), and smaller snakes.

Ring-necked snakes are secretive snakes of woodlands, plains, prairies, or even backyards. Most subspecies are absent from arid areas, but may be abundant wherever moisture occurs. Expect to find these snakes on seasonally damp hillsides, in moist canyons, along riparian corridors, in the proximity of permanent or semipermanent lakes and ponds, or along artificial water retention facilities, such as irrigation canals. Search for ring-necks beneath flat rocks and dried cow patties, or behind bark-shards on both standing and fallen trees. As an area dries, a ring-neck will nudge its way into moisture-retaining decomposing logs, or, where soil conditions allow, burrow or follow deepening soil cracks rather deeply. They may be found from sea level to an altitude of about 7,200 feet.

When startled, subspecies having bright red orange subcaudal color coil the tail tightly and elevate it. It is thought that this aposematic coloration may indicate a degree of unpalatability to predators. Certainly some predators have been known to eat, then regurgitate ring-necked snakes, or to bite, then release the snakes and wipe their mouths against grasses or sand as if trying to rid themselves of an unpleasant taste. However, other predators, coral snakes among them, readily eat ring-necked snakes with no sign of distress.

Large female ring-necks may produce up to 10 eggs. Incubation durations are variable, but probably average about 7 weeks. The hatchlings are about 5 inches in length.

The Ring-necked Ones

I was on a ring-necked snake (*Diadophis punctatus* ssp.) photographing kick. Since the Pacific Coast is the ring-neck capital of the world (with six described but questionably valid subspecies), it only made sense (to me, at least) to make a jaunt from San Diego, California, to mid-Oregon and take pictures of all ring-necks found along the way. Even as I started westward I questioned what my success rate would be, for the Pacific Coast ring-necks are traditionally surface active during the spring, then go far beneath the surface as the days get hotter and drier. It was already late April and other field herpers had cautioned me that surface conditions were quickly becoming intolerable for these little gray snakes with the red orange belly and neck band.

Three days after leaving Florida I was ready to start. My proposed route took me northward from San Diego as far as was needed to find all subspecies of the snake.

One by one I succeeded. The San Diego ring-neck was found and photographed. It looked as though I was about to fail with the San Bernardino subspecies, but Brad Alexander had a gorgeous specimen that he allowed me to photograph. Next came the Monterey form (no problem there), and a few hours later I found a Pacific ring-neck. That left me two to go. I actually found a northwestern ring-neck in northern California. That find allowed me to turn around well south of my intended northern limitation in central Oregon.

continued

Now it was necessary to go inland to the Sierra Nevadas in search of the coral-bellied ring-neck, the last of the Pacific forms and the one that I wished most to see.

Gerold Merker took me under his tutelage and together we visited a coral-bellied ring-neck denning site. It was wonderful. There were boards, sheets of tin, and flat surface rocks galore. It was undoubtedly a ring-neck paradise—but the problem was, there were no ring-necks.

Gerold and I searched the area for more than an hour. We found western yellow-bellied racers, skinks, and alligator lizards, but nary a ring-neck. Gerold was mortified. Never before had he looked for the snake and not found at least one. But so goes the hobby of field herping. As they say, "win some, lose some."

Even without the coral-bellied ring-neck I considered the trip a resounding success. When traveling through country as picturesque as the Sierras, whether or not herps are found, it is impossible to truly lose.

And it turned out that, thanks to Rick Staub, who just happened to have a coral-bellied ring-neck in hand, I was able to complete the photographic record of the Pacific Coast subspecies before returning to the east. Two years later I actually found a coral-bellied ring-neck in the field. The search was completed.

79–86. Ring-necked Snake
Diadophis punctatus

Abundance/Range: Abundant but often seasonally active. Collectively, this snake is found from central Washington to northwestern Baja. It occurs also from southeastern Colorado to (and beyond) the Mexican border, and westward to central Arizona. Disjunct populations are known in eastern Washington, Idaho, Oregon, Nevada, Arizona, and Utah. Check the range map.

Habitat: On the seasonally dry southern Pacific coast this abundant snake is surface active during cool weather when the soils are damp from the

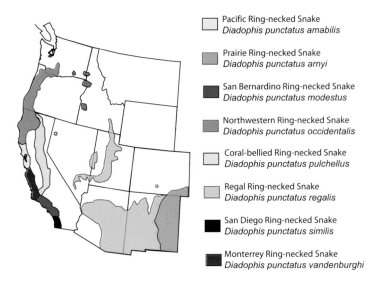

Pacific Ring-necked Snake
Diadophis punctatus amabilis

Prairie Ring-necked Snake
Diadophis punctatus arnyi

San Bernardino Ring-necked Snake
Diadophis punctatus modestus

Northwestern Ring-necked Snake
Diadophis punctatus occidentalis

Coral-bellied Ring-necked Snake
Diadophis punctatus pulchellus

Regal Ring-necked Snake
Diadophis punctatus regalis

San Diego Ring-necked Snake
Diadophis punctatus similis

Monterrey Ring-necked Snake
Diadophis punctatus vandenburghi

winter rains. In other areas it is active on cool foggy or rainy nights. It is most common near watercourses and springs and at the edges of damp meadows.

Size: Although the adults of some of the larger races may attain a length of 30 inches, it is seldom that any western race, other than the regal ring-neck, exceeds 18 inches. The regal ring-neck may rather regularly attain 24 inches or more in total length and has a record size of 33½ inches.

Identifying features: Because of intergradation and color plasticity we suggest that if you wish to identify a ring-necked snake to subspecies, use range as a primary identification tool.

All races of the ring-necked snake are steel olive to steel gray or powder gray above and coral orange to pale orange, with or without dark flecks or spots, ventrally. Of the western races only the regal ring-neck routinely lacks the namesake ring around the neck.

Ring-necks have round pupils, 15 (occasionally 17) rows of smooth scales at midbody and divided anal plates.

Check the individual subspecies accounts below (79–86) for additional information.

Similar snakes: Black-headed snakes have white(ish) neck rings. Brown and red-bellied snakes have keeled scales.

Pacific Ring-necked Snake

SUBSPECIES

79. The Pacific Ring-necked Snake, *D. p. amabilis*, is found in the coastal mountain ranges and their adjacent regions. This ring-neck ranges southward from northern San Francisco Bay to the vicinity of Monterey Bay, California.

The yellowish orange to orange belly is rather sparsely speckled with black. The subcaudal scales are bright red. The ventral color ascends onto the fawn, olive, or blue black sides for ½–1½ scale rows. The orange neck band is narrow, being only 1–1½ scale rows wide. This subspecies is adult at 10½–16 inches in length.

80. The Prairie Ring-necked Snake, *D. p. arnyi*, is widespread in our central states. It occurs from south central Texas, northward to northern Iowa, and westward to central New Mexico and southeastern Colorado. The neck-ring is wide and well defined, but may break on the nape. The dorsum can vary from olive gray to olive. The belly is orange and patterned with (often) paired, but well-separated, black half-moons. The orange of the venter seldom extends upward onto even the lowest row of lateral scales. The subcaudal scales are bright red. This race is adult at 10–13 inches in length, with a record size of 16½ inches.

Prairie Ring-necked Snake

81. The San Bernardino Ring-necked Snake, *D. p. modestus*, is found in coastal areas from the vicinity of Santa Barbara, California, to the Los Angeles area. This is a rather dark race of ring-neck and the (often) narrow neckband (½–2 scales wide) does not always strongly contrast with the body color. The belly color is a bright orange to orange red. Most ventral scutes have four conspicuous black spots, one at each outer edge

San Bernardino Ring-necked Snake

Northwestern Ring-necked Snake

and two more centrally. The orange ventral coloration extends upward, encompassing the bottom half of the lowermost row of lateral scales. The subcaudal scales are bright red.

82. In the states of Oregon and Washington, where it is the only race of ring-necked snake to occur, subspecific identification of the Northwestern Ring-necked Snake, *D. p. occidentalis*, is a simple matter. More care in identification will be needed where its range abuts those of other races in northern California. From the Cascade Range of Washington, this snake ranges southward to Sonoma County, California. The dorsal scales are grayish green to olive. The chin is heavily speckled. The neck ring is 1–3 scales wide, the venter is reddish orange, and the subcaudals are brilliant red. Each ventral scute bears 1 prominent black spot, sometimes 2. The bright ventral color extends upward onto the sides for ½–2 full scale rows. Black flecks may also occur on these lowermost scale rows. Although it is known to attain a full 2 feet in length, most northwestern ring-necked snakes are adult at 11–18 inches.

83. The Coral-bellied Ring-necked Snake, *D. p. pulchellus*, is one of the more brilliantly colored races. It occurs on the western slopes of Califor-

Coral-bellied Ring-necked Snake

nia's Sierra Nevadas. It is quite similar in appearance to the northwestern ring-necked snake, differing principally in usually having an immaculate orange ventral color and in lacking black flecks on the lowermost 2 rows of lateral scales. The adult size seems to be between 11 and 16 inches.

84. The Regal Ring-necked Snake, *D. p. regalis*, is the largest, palest, and most arid-adapted subspecies. Although it can attain sexual maturity at 10–16 inches in length, this pretty snake has a record size of 33½ inches. It seeks the dampest areas (riparian corridors, the environs of stock tanks, etc.) in semiarid grasslands and thornscrub and is often absent from truly arid areas. The regal ring-necked snake may be found from southeastern Idaho southward to central Texas and Mexico, and from central eastern Nevada to western Arizona, and possibly into the region of Death Valley, California. This is one of the most distinctively colored of the ring-necks. The dorsal color is pale ash gray, olive gray, or olive. The belly is yellowish to pale orange. There are 4 rows of well-defined dark black spots on each ventral scute. The central 2 rows are the most prominent. The yellow ventral color often includes the lowest of the lateral scale rows. The underside of the tail is quite a bright red. The neck ring may be well defined, poorly defined, or entirely absent. There are 17 scale rows.

Regal Ring-necked Snake, nonring-necked phase

Regal Ring-necked Snake, ring-necked phase

San Diego Ring-necked Snake

85. The San Diego Ring-necked Snake, *D. p. similis*, has a rather small range, occurring primarily in San Diego County, California, and adjacent Baja California. It is also known from southwestern San Bernardino County. It has 15 scale rows and heavy dark markings at the outermost edge of each ventral scute, but otherwise poorly defined ventral spotting. The central spots may adjoin the outermost ones to form a single prominent row along each side of the venter. The orange of the venter includes at least part of the first row of lateral scales. The subcaudal scales are bright red. Each chin and lower labial scale bears a dark spot. The neck ring may be well defined or rather pale, and is 1½–3 scales wide. The dorsum may vary from olive to a rather dark gray, and be darker laterally than middorsally.

86. The Monterey Ring-necked Snake, *D. p. vandenburghi* is restricted to the coastal ranges and adjacent habitats, from Santa Cruz County, California, southward to Ventura County. The neck ring is 1½–2½ scale rows wide. The back can vary from yellowish green to olive gray. The ventral color is brighter than that of many subspecies, being red anteriorly and an even brighter red posteriorly and beneath the tail. The ventral color extends upward, including all of the first row of scales and the lower half of the second row. The dark ventral spotting is poorly defined.

Monterey Ring-necked Snake

Fangless Night Snakes, Genus *Hypsiglena*

Taxonomic note: Depending on the authority quoted, the wide-ranging night snake is represented in the western United States either by a single randomly variable species, by a single species having six diagnosable subspecies, or by three species containing a total of six subspecies. We will adopt the latter concept here.

The single best-developed identifying characteristic is the presence of two or three large neck blotches (which may rarely be entirely absent). The number of these, their comparative size, and their general shape may help differentiate the species and subspecies. However, all characteristics are variable, so we urge you to also consider range when attempting identification. Night snakes are profusely spotted both dorsally and laterally. The dorsal ground color (the color between the dorsal spots) is often considerably lighter than the lateral ground color and usually closely matches the substrate on which the snakes are found. All have a dark horizontal bar through the eye that often is in contact with the nuchal blotch. The venter is an immaculate white.

Night snakes are small and preferentially nocturnal, and have vertically elliptical pupils. The body scale rows are either 19 or 21. The scales are smooth; the anal plate is divided. This snake seldom attempts to bite. Lizards are the preferred prey, but small frogs and their larvae, smaller snakes, and some invertebrates are also eaten. While captives have accepted newly born mice, it is not known whether specimens in the wild do so. The toxic saliva benumbs and kills the prey rather quickly.

This is an oviparous species. A clutch can contain up to 11 eggs, but 3–6 is the norm. Incubation lasts 50–65 days. Hatchlings are about 7 inches long.

These secretive snakes emerge from hiding as the daylight wanes, and may be active far into the night. They are primarily terrestrial and may be quite common in areas where flat rocks, cactus skeletons, or other surface debris provides ample surface cover.

Depending on the subspecies and the terrain in which it occurs, night snakes may be found from sea level to altitudes of more than 8,500 feet.

87. Sonoran Night Snake

Hypsiglena chlorophaea chlorophaea

Abundance/Range: This common snake ranges southward from northern Arizona, throughout most of that state, to northwestern mainland Mexico.

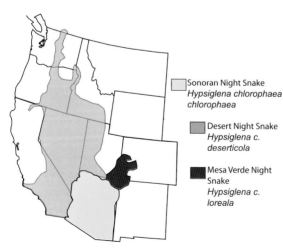

Sonoran Night Snake
Hypsiglena chlorophaea chlorophaea

Desert Night Snake
Hypsiglena c. deserticola

Mesa Verde Night Snake
Hypsiglena c. loreala

Habitat: The night snakes in general are serpents of arid and semiarid lands, and are most common where surface cover, in the form of flat rocks, vegetational debris, and human-generated trash are abundantly scattered. The unused burrows of small mammals, other reptiles, and spiders are also utilized as retreats by these snakes. They may traverse

Sonoran Night Snake

considerable stretches of relatively open desert, and are one of the most frequently seen snakes on trans-desert roads at night.

Size: Most examples of this slender snake are between 8 and 12 inches in length; 16 inches would be considered a large specimen. An immense 26-inch-long specimen has been documented.

Identifying features: The ground color, and to a lesser degree, the color of the dorsal and lateral blotches and spots, usually blends well with the substrate on which these little snakes are found. This is a busily patterned but pallid race. The ground color is very light brown, grayish, tan, or cream. The light dorsal ground color extends to the sides of the darker brown dorsal blotches. The nuchal and nape blotches are very large, and usually contact each other so widely that they appear as one enlarged blotch completely crossing the neck. The head is not much wider than the neck and bears no pattern on the top. The scales are smooth and in 21 rows.

Similar species: Glossy snakes and juvenile racers have round pupils; gopher snakes have strongly keeled scales and round pupils; lyre snakes have an intricate pattern on the top of their head. Please read accounts 88–92 for discussions of other night snake species and subspecies.

Northern Desert Night Snake

ADDITIONAL SUBSPECIES

88. The Northern Desert Night Snake, *H. c. deserticola*, is another pallid desert dweller. It resembles the Sonoran race so closely that we suggest you rely on range as the identifying criterion. The dorsal spots are only slightly darker than the ground color. The nuchal blotches are very large and often contiguous; however, when the nape blotch is discernible as a separate entity, it is narrow anteriorly and greatly broadened posteriorly. This night snake ranges northward from Baja California to south central

Mesa Verde Night Snake

British Columbia in drier inland habitats. It is absent from most of the humid and rainy coastal strand.

89. The Mesa Verde Night Snake, *H. c. loreal*, is the only one of the three races to have 2 loreal scales on each side of the face. The other subspecies have only a single loreal on each side. The ground color of the back is usually noticeably lighter than that of the sides. The body scales are in 21 rows. The nuchal blotches are prominent, but the nape blotch may be lacking, represented by one or more small spots, or large and distinct. This subspecies is found throughout eastern Utah and immediately adjacent southwestern Colorado.

90. Texas Night Snake

Hypsiglena jani texana

Abundance/Range: This is the easternmost species of night snake. This common species occurs over much of Texas, Oklahoma, and New Mexico as well as southeastern Colorado and south central Kansas.

Habitat: This snake is often found among and beneath flat rocks, in boulder fields, amid vegetational debris, and under human-generated trash. It may retreat into the unused burrows of small mammals, other reptiles, or spiders. It is also often encountered in areas of sandy desert, and while crossing desert roads at night.

Size: The record size for this form is 20 inches, but most seen are 15 inches or less.

Identifying features: This is one of the larger and prettier members of the genus. This can be a stout little snake (especially when a female is carrying eggs). The 3 black neck blotches are usually well developed, large, and rounded posteriorly. The ground color—gray, olive gray, or tan—often matches the rock or sand substrate on which this snake is usually found. The 50 or more well-defined dorsal blotches are olive green to drab. The venter is white.

Similar species: Please read account numbers 88, 89, 91, and 92 for comparisons with other night snakes. Glossy snakes and juvenile racers have

Texas Night Snake

round pupils; gopher snakes have strongly keeled scales and round pupils; lyre snakes lack neck blotches. Please refer to the range maps for additional help.

91. California Night Snake

Hypsiglena ochrorhyncha nuchalata

Abundance/Range: This common snake occurs on the slopes of the Sierra Nevada and the coastal ranges near the Sacramento and San Joaquin Valleys. Look for this race southward from Shasta County to San Luis Obispo County, California.

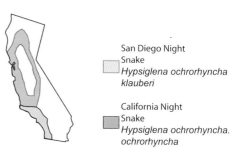

San Diego Night Snake
Hypsiglena ochrorhyncha klauberi

California Night Snake
Hypsiglena ochrorhyncha. ochrorhyncha

Habitat: Like other night snakes, the California night snake favors habitats liberally strewn with rocks and boulders. It hides beneath surface rocks, debris, and rubbish. It may also be found beneath cover on coastal grasslands, beneath fallen Joshua trees, and in other similar habitats.

California Night Snake

Size: Typically 14–16 inches in length, occasional individuals may attain a 22-inch length.

Identifying features: This newly erected species has only 19 scale rows. The nuchal blotches may contact the nape spot to form a dark band behind the head, but they are more often narrowly separated. The dark dorsal spots may alternate or be paired. If paired they may join at midline to form a single wide spot.

Similar species: Please read accounts 88, 89, 90, and 92 for comparisons with other night snakes. Glossy snakes and juvenile racers have round pupils; gopher snakes have strongly keeled scales and round pupils; lyre snakes lack neck blotches and have a dark pattern on the top of the head. Please refer to the range maps for additional help.

ADDITIONAL SUBSPECIES

92. The San Diego Night Snake, *H. o. klauberi*, has 21 scale rows. The nuchal blotches are large and broad; the nape blotch is narrow and hardly wider posteriorly than anteriorly. The ground color is variable but often a light ashy gray. The dorsal spots, dark and well defined, may be paired but are often joined vertebrally into a single wide blotch. This subspecies may

San Diego Night Snake

be found on the western slopes of the southern Sierras to the coast and from Santa Barbara County far southward onto the Baja Peninsula.

SUBFAMILY XENODONTINAE: HOG-NOSED SNAKES

Although this is a large family of rear-fanged snakes, there are only two species (one genus) of xenodontine snakes in the American west. These are the large, heavy-bodied hog-nosed snakes. Both of these snakes produce toxins that help them overcome (and perhaps predigest) their prey. Neither is known to be dangerous to humans.

Hog-noses accept amphibians (especially toads), lizards, the young of ground-nesting birds, and small mammals. It is likely that the immunity displayed by hog-nosed snakes to the venom of toads is an acquired trait.

The snakes in these two genera are oviparous. Double clutching is recorded.

Hog-noses may lay up to 25 eggs in a clutch. However, clutches are usually considerably smaller, and may contain as few as three (normally 6–15) eggs. Hatchlings emerge as 7-inch replicas of the adult.

Serpentine Bluffers

Hog-nosed snakes are the great bluffers of the American serpentine world. Deriving their common name from their strongly upturned rostral scale, three species of hog-nose in the United States are found, collectively, from the Atlantic Coast to the vicinity of Portal, Arizona, and from well south into Mexico to southern Saskatchewan, Canada.

I have never made a concerted effort to find the various subspecies of the western hog-nose, *Heterodon nasicus* ssp., in the wild, but I have been fortunate enough to happen across a few as I searched for other herp species.

For some inexplicable reason, the Mexican hog-nose has always been my favorite of the group. I say inexplicable, for the Mexican hog-nose differs only subtly from the Plains and the dusty hog-nose. The difference is in the arrangement and number of the tiny azygous scales atop the snout. The Mexican has 6 or fewer, the other races 9 or more.

All of my field experience with live Mexican hog-noses has been in western Texas, east of the scope of this guide. There I have found the snakes crossing grass-edged roadway at midday or on desert roadways at dusk. Sadly, the only one I have seen in Arizona, the westernmost extreme of the range of the subspecies, had been freshly killed by a vehicle on Route 80, somewhat south of the Portal Road.

Several of the live ones I have found chose to ignore my presence as I neared them, merely continuing on their trajectory from point A to point B. However, a few have reacted in typical hog-nose manner, flattening the body, spreading a hood, and striking with closed mouth.

Hog-noses seldom bite in defense and almost never bite in offense. However, captives (this is a popular snake with hobbyists) often have an almost savage feeding response and bites may then occur.

Hog-noses have well-developed Duvernoy's glands and rather strong toxic components in their saliva. They also have very long teeth in the rear of the upper jaw. Although its head is certainly not adapted for striking, the snake continually jerks it downward once an object is grasped, employing its elongate teeth and allowing the toxic saliva to enter the wound. Humans have had adverse reaction to bites from this snake. Hog-noses should be handled with care.

Hog-nosed Snakes, Genus *Heterodon*

Taxonomic note: Although not yet (December 2007) entirely resolved, it is thought by some researchers that all five forms of hog-nosed snakes are of sufficiently distinct lineages to be considered full species. The eastern, southern, and dusty hog-noses are extralimital. The Mexican and the Plains hog-noses occur in the area covered by this guide.

Hog-nosed snakes are famous for their defensive actions, which include huffing, puffing, writhing, and bluffing. The snakes spread a hood, flatten their head, may strike (but seldom actually bite), and, when all else fails, writhe, open their mouth, loll out their tongue to the fullest extent, and roll onto their back and play possum. They then show life only by immediately again rolling upside down if righted.

Hog-nosed snakes are particularly adept at scenting and excavating buried amphibians. Unlike the two eastern species of hog-nosed snakes, which are specialist feeders on toads, the western hog-nosed snakes routinely accept toads, lizards and small rodents.

Hog-nosed snakes have enlarged teeth in the rear of the upper jaw. However, their saliva does contain toxins, and humans who have been bitten by these snakes have experienced lividity, tenderness, and noticeable swelling at the bite site. Despite their tendency not to bite, wild hog-nosed snakes should be handled with care.

Sandy grasslands and rocky scrublands are among the preferred habitats. These snakes tend to be active by day, but during the hottest weather, the western hog-nose adopts crepuscular or nocturnal behavior patterns.

The hog-nosed snakes are stout for their length and have a moderately to prominently upturned rostral scale with a strong dorsal keel. The western forms have 23 rows of keeled body scales. The anal plate is divided.

93. Mexican Hog-nosed Snake
Heterodon kennerlyi

Abundance/Range: Although it has a wide range, the Mexican hog-nose does not seem to be particularly common in any given area. This snake is of primarily Mexican distribution. In the United States it

Mexican Hog-nosed Snake

occurs only in southeastern Arizona, southern New Mexico, and western Texas.

Habitat: Sandy prairielands and grasslands (including pastures) are preferred habitats. This snake also inhabits cactus-thornscrub semiarid lands.

Size: The Mexican hog-nose normally attains a length of 20–26 inches but may occasionally exceed 3 feet. Hatchlings are from 5¼–7 inches long.

Identifying features: This hog-nose has 9 or fewer azygous (small differentiated) scales posterior to the upturned and enlarged rostral scale. The dorsal and lateral ground color is variable and always subdued, but usually blends well with the substrate where it is found. The dorsal and lateral surfaces are usually tan, olive tan, light brown, or gray. The darker middorsal blotches are rather irregular, usually well defined, but not outlined with dark pigment. The uppermost row of lateral blotches are often round(ish), may be somewhat darker than the dorsal series, but are not outlined with darker pigment. Lower rows of lateral blotches are paler and less well defined. The top of the head is primarily dark. A poorly defined light mark outlines a dark interorbital bar, which then extends diagonally down, through the rear of each eye, to the jawline. A second dark teardrop-shaped marking extends diagonally downward from the rear of the head to the nape. The rostral scale is sharply upturned, pointed anteriorly, and keeled dorsally. The tail is short and stout. The belly is primarily dark, but bears scattered white and/or yellow orange spots. The subcaudal scales (the scales beneath the tail) are black.

Similar species: The keeled scales are in 23 rows. Except for the azygous scale count—the Mexican hog-nose has 9 or fewer, the Plains hog-nose has 10 or more—this snake is very similar to the Plains hog-nose.

94. Plains Hog-nosed Snake

Heterodon nasicus

Abundance/Range: This is a secretive but not uncommon snake. It ranges northward from southern New Mexico and northern Texas to southern Saskatchewan and southwestern Alberta. There are many narrow eastward range projections and disjunct populations to both the east and the west of the main range.

Habitat: It occurs both near and well away from temporary or permanent water sources. It takes refuge from the midday sun amid boulders, in pack rat nests, in burrows, or in other such areas of seclusion.

Size: Females, the larger sex, may attain a length of 40 inches but are usually a foot shorter. Males are adult at 14–18 inches in length.

Identifying features: The ground color is usually tan to gray, similar to the hues of the sand soils on which this snake is found, but may also be green or reddish brown. A broad dark bar runs from jawline upward through each eye and over the snout. A second, usually narrower, dark bar crosses the crown from eye to eye. A dark, diagonal, elongate patch is present on each side of the neck, and a less extensive dark marking runs rearward from the back of the head onto the nape. Subtle sexually dimor-

Plains Hog-nosed Snake

phic differences are present. Males have a dark dorsal-body-blotch count of 35 or more, while females have 40 or more blotches. The blotches contrast strongly and sharply with dorsal and lateral ground color, but may be somewhat paler than the alternating lateral blotches. There are 9 or more small (azygous) scales grouped on the snout immediately posterior to the rostral scale and between the prefrontals. The belly is predominantly black but bears scattered patches of white and/or yellow orange. The tail is short, stout, and black beneath.

Similar species: Hook-nosed snakes have smooth (nonkeeled) scales and lack a keel on the dorsal surface of the upturned rostral scale.

6

Advanced Snakes, Subfamily Natricinae

Water Snakes, Garter Snakes, Brown Snakes, and Relatives

Some researchers consider this large grouping of snakes a full family. When so considered, it is then referred to as the Natricidae. Many of the snakes in this group are semiaquatic.

American Water Snakes, Genus *Nerodia*

Although abundantly represented in the eastern United States, only three species of American water snakes are found in our west. Two are native and one is introduced. All are rather large snakes that are often very short tempered and, if restrained, quite ready to bite. If handled they are equally ready to smear an unpleasant combination of musk, feces, and urates on their captor.

As with many nonvenomous snakes, the secretions from the Duvernoy's gland are a combination of complex proteins that mix with the saliva and may prove mildly toxic to some persons. Occasional toxic reactions to the bites of closely allied genera are well documented.

All of the American water snakes are live bearing. The three western species are quite aquatic. They are heavy-bodied serpents that fishermen and hikers regularly confuse with the venomous cottonmouth, a species that does not occur in the American west. Water snakes often bask by day, even in fairly cold but sunny weather. They often choose warmed concrete abutments, protruding rocks or snags, or limbs overhanging the water as basking sites. Basking water snakes are wary and will often drop into the water and dive at the first sign of disturbance. They may surface rather quickly and may either scull slowly in place or swim parallel with the shore to assess the severity of the disturbance. If again frightened, they often submerge and remain so for long periods. Water snakes may be very active on warm, rainy or humid spring and summer nights.

Amphibians and their larvae and fish are the known foods of these snakes.

Females are usually the larger sex, and when nearing parturition can be of immense girth. Some species have more than 100 neonates in a single clutch, but 8–25 is the more normal number. The neonates are 7–12 inches in length.

Water snakes have heavily keeled, rather dull scales and, in nearly all instances, a divided anal plate. However, the several races of the plain-bellied water snake may occasionally have undivided anal plates.

95. Blotched Water Snake

Nerodia erythrogaster transversa

Abundance/Range: Throughout much of its eastern range this is an abundant snake. This does not seem to be the case in New Mexico, where it occurs only in Eddy County.
Habitat: In New Mexico, this interesting snake seems restricted to the Rio Grande, its tributaries, and some canals. It has not yet been found in stock tanks or other such water retention areas.
Size: The record size for this snake is 58 inches, but most seen are between 25 and 40 inches. Females are the larger sex.

Blotched Water Snake

Identifying features: Considerable ontogenetic changes occur in this race of the plain-bellied water snake. Neonates are prominently blotched both dorsally and laterally. Anteriorly, the lateral blotches alternate with those on the dorsum. The ground color is gray, with blotch color varying from maroon to nearly black. As the snake matures, the contrasts fade and the blotches may all but disappear. On some specimens the only dorsal markings may be in the form of short transverse bars. Mud may adhere to the heavily keeled scales, further obscuring the colors and pattern. The venter is primarily yellow, but each scute may have a vague dark marking on each side. The keeled dorsal scales are usually in 25 (23–27) rows at midbody. A great majority of the specimens have divided anal plates.

Similar snakes: Nonstriped garter snakes have undivided anal plates. The Great Plains rat snake has weakly keeled scales and is not normally aquatic. Glossy snakes have smooth scales. Gopher snakes have 4 prefrontal scales.

ADDITIONAL SUBSPECIES

There are additional races in the eastern United States as well as in Mexico.

96. Banded Water Snake (Introduced species)

Nerodia fasciata ssp.

Abundance/Range: This snake was introduced into Lake Natoma, Folsom, Sacramento County, California, where it has flourished. It has now spread to nearby bodies of permanent water.

Habitat: This big snake basks while hanging loosely in shrubs or trees overhanging the water, or while resting on protruding rocks or on the banks. It may also bask while coiled atop floating aquatic vegetation. It swims and dives readily and well.

Size: This water snake is adult at 30–48 inches. The record documented size is 60 inches. It is a heavy-bodied snake, and gravid females attain an immense girth.

Identifying features: The subspecies of banded water snake introduced to California is undetermined. It is a variable snake. Examples are banded from nape to tailtip. Some are brightly banded with dark-edged yellowish, orange, or red bands against a brownish or olive green color, while the colors of others are more muted. Even if brightly colored as a juvenile, these snakes usually dull with advancing age. Old adults may be a uniform (or almost uniform) brown dorsally. The belly is yellow to yellow olive

Banded Water Snake

and has reddish "squares" along each edge. Over time these snakes build up a residue of mud and detritus on the heavily keeled scales that further obscures pattern and color. Following the shedding of its skin (or when it is wet rather than dry) a banded water snake may appear bright and fresh. There is a dark stripe from the eye to the angle of the jaw.

Similar species: None. Nonstriped garter snakes are usually prominently checkered or spotted, not banded.

ADDITIONAL SUBSPECIES

Two additional subspecies are found in the eastern United States.

97. Northern Water Snake
Nerodia sipedon sipedon

Abundance/Range: Although common from the Atlantic seacoast westward, this snake occurs in our area only in eastern Colorado where it can be difficult to find.

Habitat: This snake occupies pond and lake shores, river and stream edges (including areas with a fair current), marsh and swamp and margins, oxbows, and possibly even temporarily flooded areas. In Colorado, it occurs at elevations below 5,500 feet. In the spring months, when nights are still cool, northern water snakes are sun worshippers, basking throughout most of the daylight hours and foraging occasionally. As temperatures increase, the snakes are able to more easily maintain a suitable body temperature, allowing them to bask less and forage more. A snake will utilize almost any exposed, fairly dry, sunlit spot to bask. Concrete or wooden bridge and dam abutments, rocks, beaver and muskrat lodges, and exposed snags and limbs overhanging the water are but a few of the possibilities. Juvenile northern water snakes are less apt than adults to come ashore to bask.

Size: Adults may be between 2 and 4½ feet long, with females the larger sex.

Identifying features: Although adults are often less brightly colored than juveniles, the northern water snake does not undergo particularly ex-

Northern Water Snake

tensive ontogenetic changes. Mud will often adhere to the keeled scales, making these snakes appear even less colorful than they actually are. To fully appreciate the brilliance and intricacy of the colors and patterns, it is often necessary to see the snake when it is either wet or, better yet, freshly shed.

The ground color of the northern water snake may be gray, buff, tan, or brown. The markings are usually much darker than the ground color, but this is not invariably so. The markings of the juveniles are often blackish, as may be those of some adults. On other examples the markings may be reddish, with or without a black border. Typically the anterior markings are in the form of rather regular, broad bands. This pattern may continue posteriorly, or the banding may change to a combination of dorsal saddles and lateral blotches. Tail bands may be regular or irregular. The belly is usually strongly patterned, but may be sparsely so, or virtually unpatterned except for a sparse to liberal dusting of dark dots. If markings are present, they may be large and in the shape of dark bordered half-moons or irregular triangles, apex directed posteriorly. They are usually arranged on each side of a complete or broken dark-edged light midline, and may be present only at the very edges of the ventral scutes. Any given specimen may combine any or all of these colors and patterns. Northern water snakes usually lack a horizontal dark ocular (eye) streak and have 21–25 scale rows. These snakes may wander widely during the rainy season. They may then be encountered crossing roadways, and well away from immediate water sources.

Similar snakes: There are no other snakes in Colorado with which you can easily confuse the northern water snake. Glossy snakes have smooth scales. Hog-nosed snakes have a prominently upturned rostral scale. Bullsnakes have a sharp nose with an enlarged rostral scale. The Great Plains rat snake has weakly keeled dorsal scales. None, except the northern water snake, are essentially aquatic.

ADDITIONAL SUBSPECIES

Three additional subspecies occur in the eastern United States.

Brown and Red-bellied Snakes, Genus *Storeria*

In the United States there are only two species in this genus of diminutive, secretive, natricine snakes. Both species are primarily of eastern distribution, have a divided anal scute, have keeled dorsal and lateral scales, and usually lack loreal scales (a scale present and situated between the preoculars and the posterior nasal scale on many other snake genera).

Red-bellied and brown snakes are ovoviviparous. A clutch contains 5–12 (rarely a few more) neonates. Neonates average about 3½ inches in length.

Depending on weather conditions, these snakes may be active day or night. Warmth and showers induce surface activity.

Slugs and earthworms are the preferred prey, but this snake also consumes small snails which it pulls from the shells as it swallows them.

While the members of this genus seldom (if ever) bite when grasped, none are loathe to void musk and/or smear feces and urates on their captor.

Only the Black Hills red-bellied snake occurs in the western United States, and the northern red-bellied snake occurs in Saskatchewan, Canada.

98. Black Hills Red-bellied Snake

Storeria occipitomaculata pahasapae

Abundance/Range: This snake is so secretive that population statistics are difficult to assess. The Black Hills red-bellied snake is currently known to occur only in central western South Dakota and adjacent Wyoming.

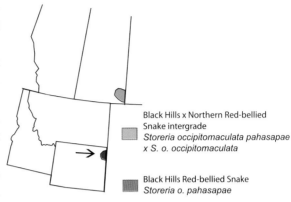

Black Hills x Northern Red-bellied
Snake intergrade
Storeria occipitomaculata pahasapae
x S. o. occipitomaculata

Black Hills Red-bellied Snake
Storeria o. pahasapae

Habitat: This snake seeks the seclusion of trash and natural cover such as fallen trees and rocks in and near moist woodlands.

Size: This tiny snake is adult at 8–11 inches in length, and only rarely attains 15 inches.

Identifying features: The dorsum is reddish brown to gray. A lighter vertebral stripe and/or four narrow dark lines may be present. The ventral coloration may be yellowish, orange red, or may, on occasion, be dark

Black Hills Red-bellied Snake

gray. This westernmost, poorly differentiated subspecies ostensibly lacks the nape and nuchal blotches and the light spot on the upper lip beneath the rear of the eye (5th upper labial). However, neither of these characteristics is constant. Neonates are darker than the adults. The dorsal scales are keeled, in 15 rows, and the anal plate is divided.

Similar snakes: None. Within its range, this is the only snake with a red belly and scales arranged in 15 rows.

ADDITIONAL SUBSPECIES

98a. The range of the red-bellied snake, an abundant snake of the eastern United States and southeastern Canada, extends westward into southeastern Saskatchewan. This northwesternmost population of red-bellied snakes is thought by some researchers to be of intergrade status between the Black Hills and the Northern subspecies, *Storeria occipitomaculata pahasapae* × *S. o. occipitomaculata*. This diminutive natricine may have a dorsal coloration of brown, reddish brown, gray, or rarely, charcoal. Often 4 thin light stripes are vaguely visible. Three light nuchal spots are usually present but may fuse into a collar or be absent. A black-bordered light marking is usually present on the 5th upper labial. The belly, normally a bright reddish orange, may occasionally be yellow, gray, or black.

Black Hills x Northern Red-bellied Snake

Garter and Ribbon Snakes, Genus *Thamnophis*

Garter snakes are among the few snake species able to coexist with humans. It may not always be easy for them, for humans often do not tolerate the presence of snakes well. But wherever they are not purposely persecuted (and sometimes even where they are), garter snakes continue to be easily found in dooryards, vacant fields, fencerows, gardens and commercial agricultural areas. Where irrigation canals draw frogs and toads, these colorful snakes may actually be abundant.

Besides amphibians, garter snakes eat worms, fish, nestlings of ground-nesting birds, and nestling rodents, frogs, and crayfish. These snakes forage both on land and in the water. Ribbon snakes prefer amphibians and fish.

Garter snakes can be remarkably hard to identify to species. To many folks, a striped snake is a striped snake—but garter snakes can be difficult for even experienced field biologists to identify. Geographic origin of the specimen can be important. Besides point of origin, such criteria as on which scale rows the lateral stripes occur, whether these stripes are straight edged or wavy, and head color may help with identification.

Garter snakes, as a group, are found in one form or another through most of the southern tier Canadian provinces southward to northern Latin America.

Most species are diurnal during the cooler weather, but may also be active at dusk and after dark during the hottest weather. Many species are associated to a greater or lesser degree with ponds or streams, and all swim and some dive well. Many seek refuge beneath submerged stones or leaves when startled.

Garter snakes have large litters of live young. The neonates of most species are 7–10 inches in length. Neonates of the aptly named giant garter snake are 9½–12 inches long, while those of the Sierra garter snake may be only 5 inches in length.

When confronted, garter snakes may flatten their head and strike savagely (ribbon snakes are more apt to just try to flee). Like their cousins, the water snakes, garter snakes have a mildly toxic saliva. If grasped, many will bite and most will smear musk, feces, and urates on their captor.

The Prettiest Garter Snake

The western states and provinces are short on water snakes but long on garter snakes—and among the latter are some of the most beautiful snakes in the world, as well as some that are dishwater dull. These are no less interesting, just dull in color.

Gary Nafis and I were photographing San Francisco alligator lizards, *Elgaria c. coerulea*, in an area north of the Bay where there were a few boards and many fallen trees as cover. It was an ideal area for the alligator lizards. We had found numerous neonates and were hoping for a larger one to complete the photo quest. The fog cover was still dense when we arrived. But now, through the fog, we could see the late spring sun as a yellow orb. Within the hour the fog would give way to Sol's evaporating rays and the landscape would heat quickly.

Finally a warming ray illuminated a long-fallen limb, and almost immediately a serpentine form emerged from beneath the limb and coiled quietly in the grass. I glanced at it and did a double take. It was a California red-sided garter snake, *Thamnophis sirtalis infernalis*, a snake with which I was quite familiar, but I had never seen one with the color intensity of the snake before me. The dorsolateral spots from which the snake takes its common name and the crown of the head were an intense coral red. The dorsal and lateral stripes were a chalk white, and the black was an ebony.

Spectacular?

You bet! In my opinion, only the endangered San Francisco garter snake, *T. s. tetrataenia*, can near this subspecies in beauty.

99. Santa Cruz Garter Snake

Thamnophis atratus atratus

Taxonomic note: Collectively, the three sub-species of this garter snake are referred to as aquatic garter snakes.

Abundance/Range: *T. a. atratus* can be relatively common in areas of suitable habitat. Because of its affiliation for rocky streams, it cannot be considered a generally distributed species. This race ranges from the southern San Francisco Bay area to the Santa Cruz Mountains.

Santa Cruz Garter Snake
Thamnophis a. atratus

Diablo Range Garter Snake
Thamnophis a. zaxanthus

Oregon Garter Snake
Thamnophis a. hydrophilus

Habitat: The Santa Cruz garter snake is highly aquatic and associated with rocky sections of creeks, streams, and ponds. It is a strong swimmer, and if startled on shore it will readily take to the water. It dives well and can remain submerged for several minutes.

Size: The Santa Cruz garter snake may near 36 inches in length, but most are between 18 and 28 inches in length. They are of moderate girth.

Santa Cruz Garter Snake

Identifying features: This garter snake has a ground color that is usually very dark (dark brown to black), usually with two rows of small, alternating dark lateral spots. Short lengthwise patches of white interstitial skin are often visible. The butter yellow (occasionally orangish) vertebral stripe is prominent and well defined. The lateral stripes are very pale to absent. The Santa Cruz garter snake often has a bright yellow throat. It has 8 upper and (usually) 11 lower labial scales narrowly barred with dark pigment along their vertical sutures. None of the labial scales are greatly enlarged. The belly is bluish or greenish and may bear pinkish or yellowish smudges. The keeled scales are in 19 rows at midbody; the anal plate is not divided.

Similar species: The various races of the common garter snake have 7 upper labial scales. The four races of the western terrestrial garter snake have 8 upper labials with numbers 6 and 7 enlarged; these labial scales are also often higher than wide.

ADDITIONAL SUBSPECIES

100. Despite having a greater range in California than in its namesake state, the northern race of this species is referred to as the Oregon Garter Snake, *T. a. hydrophilus*. It ranges northward from the vicinity of northern Sonoma County, California, to Douglas County, Oregon.

Oregon Garter Snake

The Oregon garter snake is less brightly colored and precisely marked than the Santa Cruz race. The ground color of this race varies from a rather olive tan or pale gray to olive gray or olive black. The lateral and vertebral stripes may be present or lacking. When present they may be quite well defined, but often do not contrast sharply with the ground color. There are usually two rows of alternating dark spots present on each side. These are most visible on snakes with the lighter ground colors. Light interstitial skin may be visible both laterally and dorsally. The Oregon garter snake often has 21 rows of scales at midbody.

101. The Diablo Range Garter Snake, *T. a. zaxanthus*, has had a checkered taxonomic history. It was at one time erroneously recognized as *T. couchii aquaticus*. It is still not recognized as a separate entity by many researchers, being instead considered a three-striped morph of *T. a. atratus* or an intergrade between the Santa Cruz and the Oregon garter snakes. This garter snake has a relatively narrow head. The ground color is gray, olive brown, brown, or black. Lateral spots darker than the ground color may be present and are most visible on young snakes and when the snake is wet or freshly shed. The yellow to orange vertebral stripe is broad and well defined. The greenish lateral stripes are somewhat less prominent and on scale rows 2 and 3. The belly is predominantly bluish or greenish and may bear lighter patches centrally having a pinkish or yellowish tinge. The

Diablo Range Garter Snake

snake is found from Santa Barbara County northward to Napa and Solano counties, north and east of San Francisco. It is often, but not invariably, associated with rocky bottomed creeks, streams, and other bodies of water.

102. Sierra Garter Snake

Thamnophis couchii

Abundance/Range: This is not an uncommon snake, but it is alert and may be difficult to approach. *T. couchii* occurs in eastern central California and western Nevada.

Habitat: This is a snake that may be found in habitats as varied as cold mountain streams and pools, or warmer low-elevation pond and reservoir edges. It prefers areas with vegetation on which it may bask, as well as jumbled rocks and boulders both at waterside and submerged. This snake occurs from near sea level to elevations of more than 7,500 feet in the Sierra Nevadas.

Size: Although it is usually considerably smaller, the Sierra garter snake occasionally attains 4 feet in length; however, most seen are between 18 and 34 inches long.

Identifying features: The ground color of this dark garter snake varies from olive gray, to olive black, to olive brown. Northern, southern, and

Sierra Garter Snake

"plain" color phases have been identified. All have dark, elongate neck blotches, but these may be difficult to see.

The northern morph has three poorly defined yellowish white stripes and two rows of small, alternating dark spots on a ground color of olive green. There is black mottling on the labial scales and chin shields, and usually on the venter.

The southern morph is basically a two-toned snake—olive black dorsally and whitish ventrally. The vertebral stripe is barely visible, but is usually best defined anteriorly. The alternating black spots are present, but barely visible against the dark ground color. Much, or even all, of the black labial, chin, and ventral mottling is lacking.

The plain morph has very poorly defined stripes and spots on an olive brown ground color. The venter is quite yellow. It is found near the central portion of the range.

Melanism is not at all uncommon in this garter snake.

This is a small-eyed, narrow-snouted garter snake. It has 8 upper labial scales, with number 6 (counting backward along the lip from the snout) being the largest. The Sierra garter snake usually has 21 rows of keeled scales at midbody, but southern specimens may have only 19 rows. The anal plate is not divided.

Similar species: Other garter snakes within the range of this species have prominent vertebral stripes.

ADDITIONAL SUBSPECIES

None.

103. Western Black-necked Garter Snake

Thamnophis cyrtopsis cyrtopsis

Abundance/Range: This remains a rather common snake throughout much of its range; however, it is adept at hiding, so it may be easily overlooked. This pretty garter snake ranges westward from Texas' Big Bend region (intergrades between this and the eastern black-necked garter snake occur even farther to the east) through much of New

Western Black-necked Garter Snake

Mexico, southern Colorado, and parts of eastern and central Arizona. It also occurs far southward in Mexico.

Habitat: The black-necked garter snake invades many semiarid and aridland habitats, but is usually associated with ponds, streams, rivers, or stock tanks. During the rainy season, it may wander far afield. It prefers rock-strewn hillsides, riverbeds, wooded canyons, and even cactus-succulent associations. Following the rains, as aridland pools and ponds dry, this snake often follows the retreat of the waters to more permanent water sources. During the hot days of summer, the western black-necked garter snake becomes quite aquatic, and may be found floating on the water surface or on floating plant mats. Despite its aquatic tendencies, this species does not frequently dive.

Size: Although most specimens found are between 18 and 30 inches in length, a specimen of 42³⁄₁₆ inches has been authenticated.

Identifying features: This is a dark but pretty garter snake. The dorsal coloration is grayish brown, olive brown, dark brown, or nearly black. The vertebral and lateral stripes (the latter are on scale rows 2 and 3) are well defined and of a whitish yellow to yellow or tan in color. All stripes are apt to be brightest anteriorly. Between the lateral and the vertebral stripes, there are 2 alternating rows of large black spots. These may contrast sharply with the ground color, or be barely discernible. A pair of black blotches is on the neck. These usually have rounded posterior margins. The top of the head is brownish gray or bluish gray. There are 7 or 8 upper labials. The vertical labial sutures are dark. The belly is pale blue, pale brown, or vaguely greenish. The dorsal scales are keeled, in 19 rows at midbody, and the anal plate is not divided. This is a rather mild-mannered garter snake that is usually reluctant to bite, and if handled gently, may not even indulge in the disconcerting (and normal) garter snake ploy of voiding and smearing the cloacal contents on its captor.

Similar species: The neck blotches of the checkered garter snake, the species most similar to the black-necked, are often proportionately larger and more squared posteriorly than the more rounded ones of the black-neck. The checkered garter snake has a yellow crescent posterior to the corner of the mouth and 21 scale rows at midbody. Other sympatric garter snake species have a pale vertebral stripe, lack the neck blotches, or both. Patch-nosed snakes and whipsnakes have smooth scales and divided anal plates.

ADDITIONAL SUBSPECIES

An eastern and a Mexican race are also recognized.

WESTERN TERRESTRIAL GARTER SNAKES

104. Mountain Garter Snake

Thamnophis elegans elegans

Taxonomic note: Collectively, the three subspecies of this garter snake are referred to by the somewhat misleading name of terrestrial garter snakes. Although all races may wander far from standing water, especially in more arid areas of their

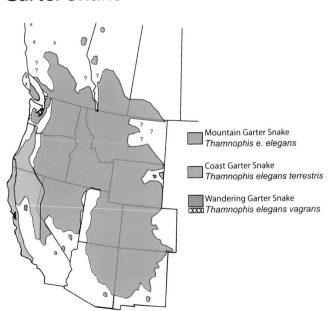

Mountain Garter Snake
Thamnophis e. elegans

Coast Garter Snake
Thamnophis elegans terrestris

Wandering Garter Snake
Thamnophis elegans vagrans

Mountain Garter Snake

range they are often found in and near beaver ponds, marshes, streams, springs, and other water sources.

Abundance: This snake may be uncommon in some areas, but relatively common in optimum habitat. This race inhabits most of central California (excluding the coast) and immediately adjacent western Nevada.

Habitat: Although it is often found in the proximity of water, the mountain garter snake also wanders far afield. This is especially so during the rainy season. It is found from verdant mountain valleys to the proximity of aridland stock tanks, and in most habitats between. This snake prefers heavily vegetated areas, and can be common where pondside grasses and emergent rushes are thick. It utilizes vegetation and logs as natural cover, but also takes advantage of human-generated debris. Although most common at lower elevations (sea level to 7,500 feet) examples of the mountain garter snake have been found as high as 13,200 feet!

Size: Although an occasional specimen may attain 3½ feet in length, the more normal size is between 16 and 30 inches.

Identifying features: This is one of the prettier and more precisely patterned of this clan. The dorsum is usually olive black to black, but may also be gray or grayish brown. All three stripes are usually well defined (they may be suffused by melanin in some very dark examples), but the lateral stripes may be somewhat paler than the vertebral stripe. Both vertebral and lateral stripes are about 2 scale rows wide (vertebral follows the contours of a full row of scales bordered by ½ row on each side). The stripe color is often whitish or butter yellow, but may be of some shade of orange. The belly is pale yellow, sometimes darker centrally, sometimes smudged with darker pigment.

The 8 upper labials and 3 prominent stripes and very dark ground color will differentiate the mountain garter snakes from many sympatric garter snake species and subspecies.

Similar species: The Santa Cruz garter snake lacks red on the sides and venter. Other sympatric garter snakes often lack well developed stripes. The various races of the common garter snake have 7 upper labial scales. The checkered garter snake has bigger and better-defined dark body spots, and both it and the black-necked garter snake have proportionately large and well-defined nuchal blotches. Patch-nosed and whipsnakes have smooth scales and a divided anal plate.

ADDITIONAL SUBSPECIES

105. The Coast Garter Snake, *T. e. terrestris*, is quite variable in color. The dorsal ground color may be russet, brown, or black. There is a tendency for the more brightly colored examples to be from the San Francisco Bay area. Northern examples may be olive or russet; those from the southern

Coast Garter Snake

Coast Garter Snake, orange phase

part of the range have a black dorsum. Some examples have the white to yellow stripes well defined (this is especially so on the reddish specimens), but other specimens may have the lateral stripes less prominent than the vertebral stripe. There are usually 2 rows of alternating but well-separated dark spots between the vertebral and the lateral lines. Some specimens may have red and black barred sides. Even dark specimens may have some orange scales on the side. The belly may have reddish spots or blotches on a field of pale yellow to bluish yellow. The throat is pale. This race ranges southward from the vicinity of Coos County, Oregon, to Santa Barbara County, California.

106. The Wandering Garter Snake, *T. e. vagrans*, has a range larger than all other races combined. It occurs from Vancouver Island, British Columbia, in the northwest and southwestern Saskatchewan in the northeast, southward to central California, northern Arizona, and northern New Mexico.

The races once known as the Arizona (*T. e. arizonae*) and the Upper Basin (*T. e. vascotanneri*) garter snakes have again been synonymized with the wandering garter snake, *T. e. vagrans*.

Wandering Garter Snake, eastern Arizona locale

Wandering Garter Snake, north central Colorado phase

The wandering garter snake is a variably colored race, and may be black with well-defined striping in the northwestern part of its range, or gray or grayish brown with striping faint or lacking farther to the east and south. Lateral stripes may be well or poorly defined. There are two rows of dark lateral spots. Because of intrusion of the dark pigment from the upper row of dark lateral spots, the vertebral stripe (which is narrow) may appear wavy, or actually be broken. The pattern definition may appear hazy. This is an abundant and commonly seen snake.

In western Washington and western British Columbia, the wandering garter snake is of very dark ground color. There the stripes tend to be narrow, have irregular edges, and be suffused with some additional scattered scales or patches of dark pigment.

Because of its variability, this race can be problematic to identify. The various races of the common garter snake have 7 rather than 8 upper labials. Checkered and black-necked garter snakes have prominent nuchal blotches. The fact that the wandering garter snake often has a "hazy" pattern and/or a wavy vertebral stripe will differentiate it from many other forms.

Besides the three races in the United States, a fourth race, *Thamnophis elegans hueyi*, occurs in northern Baja California.

107. Northern Mexican Garter Snake

Thamnophis eques megalops

Abundance/Range: This snake is of very restricted distribution in the United States, but, where found, it can be relatively common. In the United States, this species occurs in several disjunct regions of Arizona and in central western New Mexico.

Habitat: Like most garter snakes, this species is associated with aquatic habitats. It is often found in montane canyons and woodlands but is also present at lower elevations. It may be found near water in grasslands, mesquite thickets, and along desert watercourses. In some areas it seems most common in the environs of stock tanks, but prefers those surrounded by dense ground vegetation and having stands of emergents such as cattails growing near the shore.

Northern Mexican Garter Snake. Photo by Andy Holycross

Size: Most commonly seen at lengths of 18–30 inches, the northern Mexican garter snake is known to reach 40 inches in length.

Identifying features: This is a rather brightly colored, three-striped form of garter snake. The ground color is olive gray to dark olive brown or olive black. A pair of moderately large dark nuchal blotches may be distinct, or may blend almost imperceptibly posteriorly with the ground color. Three rows of black spots—2 alternating rows between the lateral and the vertebral stripes, and one beneath the lateral stripe—are present. They are easily visible on snakes with a light ground color, but less distinct on dark-colored snakes. The vertebral stripe is often wide, involving the entire vertebral scale row and about ½ of each paravertebral row. The lateral stripe is on scale rows 3 and 4 anteriorly, and drops to rows 2 and 3 posteriorly. There is a short, but usually wide-based light crescent behind the mouth. The 8 supralabials have dark vertical sutures. The keeled dorsal scales are usually in 19 (more rarely 21) rows at midbody; the anal plate is not divided.

Similar species: The placement of the lateral stripe on the Northern Mexican garter snake (3rd and 4th scale row anteriorly and 2nd and 3rd row posteriorly) and the limited range in the United States should adequately identify this species.

ADDITIONAL SUBSPECIES

There are two additional Mexican subspecies.

108. Giant Garter Snake

Thamnophis gigas

Abundance/Range: Because of habitat degradation, this interesting snake has dwindled in numbers. It may still be locally common, but has been extirpated over large sections of its range. It is now considered a threatened species by both the state of California and the federal government. This gargantuan garter snake is restricted in range to the San Joaquin and Sacramento valleys of the state of California. Its historic continuous range has now been divided into a northern and a southern population. One has as its southernmost point the San Francisco Bay area (San Joaquin County) and ranges from there northward to the vicinity of Butte County. The second population ranges southward from the vicinity of Merced County to Kern County.

Giant Garter Snake

Habitat: This is a very aquatic snake that is associated with water-edge habitats. It may be seen in marshes, in irrigation canals, and along slow streams, and is most often found where emergent vegetation is thick and matted. The giant garter snake may often be seen basking on recumbent stems and leaves of emergent plants, as well as on overhanging boughs of willows and other waterside shrubs.

Size: With a record size of 65 inches, this is indeed a giant among its brethren! More typically, however, adults vary between 36 and 48 inches in length.

Identifying features: This snake occurs in two distinctly different color/pattern morphs, which are actually just variations of the same theme. One is olive black striped with yellow. The other is a dark olive on light olive checkerboard pattern.

The striped morph has a deep olive black ground color, but in good light, evidence of checkerboarding can still usually be seen. The vertebral and lateral stripes may be a rather bright yellow and well defined, or relatively pale and more poorly defined. The lateral stripe involves scale rows 2 and 3.

The checkerboard pattern is more pronounced on snakes with paler ground color (the checkers remain dark) and striping. In some cases the stripes may be virtually absent.

Both variations have a brown(ish) venter and a light throat.

There are usually 8 upper labial scales that are barred along their vertical sutures. And, although it is difficult to discern field characteristics, the 6th upper labial scale is shorter (from front suture to rear) than the 7th. There may be either 21 or 23 scale rows. The anal plate is not divided.

Similar snakes: Other garter snakes can be quite similar to the giant garter snake in appearance and may require close examination to differentiate. The subspecies of the common garter snake usually have 7 upper labial scales and proportionately large eyes. The western aquatic garter snake can be very similar to the giant garter snake in appearance. However, the 6th upper labial of the former is longer (from front suture to rear) than the 7th.

ADDITIONAL SUBSPECIES

None.

109. Two-striped Garter Snake

Thamnophis hammondii

Abundance/Range: This garter snake is now protected by the state of California. Many of its traditional habitats have been drained, or are suffering seriously reduced flow because of diversion for irrigation. This has resulted in the decline and/or extirpation of many populations of this snake. The home of this rather aquatic garter snake extends southward from Monterey Bay, California (largely west of the Diablo and Tremblor Ranges), to northern Baja California.

Habitat: This is another of California's primarily aquatic garter snakes. It occurs along streams, flooded ditches, and in the vicinity of stock tanks and other permanent water. It is most frequently encountered where streamside (and streambed) rocks are prevalent where streams pass through chaparral, oak and pine woodlands.

Size: This garter snake is of moderate size. Adults have been known to attain 36 inches in length, but are more often between 18 and 30 inches.

Two-striped Garter Snake

Identifying features: The two-striped garter snake occurs in two pattern morphs. Both morphs have an olive drab to olive brown, or gray dorsal color. Neither morph has a vertebral stripe; however, one has well to poorly developed yellowish to gray lateral stripes on scale rows 2 and 3, while the second lacks even vestiges of the lateral stripes. Although both variations have dark spots in 2 or 4 rows, the striped morph tends to have a more uniformly colored dorsum, while the nonstriped variation has 2 rows of poorly defined dark spots on each side. The belly varies from a nearly unmarked pale yellow to butter yellow or even orange with dark smudging. The throat is light. The 8 supralabials (as well as the infralabials) are prominently barred along their vertical sutures. Supralabial 6 and 7 are roughly the same length. The keeled scales are usually in 19 rows at midbody; the anal plate is single.

Similar species: The common garter snake usually has 7 supralabial scales. Other garter snakes within the range of this species usually have a vertebral stripe. See also account 102 for a discussion of the Sierra garter snake and account 108 for the giant garter snake, two species that may lack the vertebral stripe.

ADDITIONAL SUBSPECIES

None.

110. Marcy's Checkered Garter Snake

Thamnophis marcianus marcianus

Abundance/Range: Although there are no data to substantiate a cyclic fluctuation in numbers, the checkered garter snake seems more common some years than others. Most populations seem secure, and as irrigation stretches farther and farther into the desertlands, the range of the checkered garter snake does likewise. In the United States this snake ranges westward from central Texas and extreme south central Kansas to central New Mexico and south central Arizona. It is also found in southwestern Arizona and adjacent southeastern California, but seems absent from

Marcy's Checkered Garter Snake

the harshest areas of the Sonoran Desert. Its range extends far southward into mainland Mexico.

Habitat: This is a grassland, semiarid- and aridland species. Although the checkered garter snake may wander rather far from water, especially during the monsoons, it is most often found in rather close proximity to irrigation canals, streams, stock tanks, ponds, and other water sources.

Size: With a normal length of 20–28 inches, this species is an average-sized garter snake. Occasionally a specimen three feet long will be found, and the record size is a heavy-bodied 42½ inches. Males tend to be smaller and slenderer than females.

Identifying features: This is one of the prettiest of the garter snakes. The dorsal ground color is usually some shade of tan, and both the lateral and vertebral stripes are usually well in evidence. The lateral stripe is usually restricted to scale row 3. Each side, between the lateral and the vertebral stripes, is prominently checkered with a double row of large, black spots. The top edge of the dorsal-most blotches encroaches slightly on the edges of the vertebral stripe, producing a slightly uneven appearance. There is a large dark neck blotch on each side, and a pale crescent is present at the rear of the mouth. The top of the head is olive brown to brown. The belly is usually light (whitish or yellow) and can be either unmarked or smudged with darker pigment. The keeled dorsal scales are in 21 rows at midbody and the anal plate is undivided.

Similar species: The large black neck blotches are shared in the United States only by the black- necked and northern Mexican garter snakes. The blotches and the strongly checkered body pattern will eliminate most other garter snakes. The northern Mexican garter snake has the lateral stripes on scale rows 3 and 4 anteriorly. The black-necked garter snake has a less well-defined yellow crescent at the corner of the mouth.

ADDITIONAL SUBSPECIES

There are two additional Mexican subspecies.

111. Northwestern Garter Snake
Thamnophis ordinoides

Abundance/Range: The pretty and variable northwestern garter snake is a common to abundant species of our Pacific states. It can be particularly abundant in suburban vacant lots. On an island in Puget Sound, in one small building lot containing long discarded construction materials, more than 50 northwestern garter snakes (plus a dozen or more Puget Sound garter snakes) were found! It ranges northward from northern California onto Vancouver Island and the adjacent mainland of British Columbia, Canada.

Habitat: This species is a damp meadow and woodland clearing snake. It continues to persist in the immediate proximity of humans, and can be particularly common in debris-laden vacant lots. It is adept at hiding beneath boards, roofing tin, logs, grass mats, and other surface cover. In these habitats it occurs sympatrically with other garter snake species. This snake is diurnally active, but may move at dusk or early evening, when temperatures are suitable. This species may be found from sea level to elevations of 4,500 feet.

Size: Although exceptional specimens may exceed 3 feet in total length, between 20 and 24 inches is the more common adult size.

Identifying features: The ground color of this narrow-headed garter snake may be tan, olive, brown, or black and the middorsal stripe may

Northwestern Garter Snake

Northwestern Garter Snake

vary from being well defined along the entire length of the snake to being entirely absent. If present, it is usually best defined anteriorly. The stripe color may vary from blue, to white, through yellow, to a rather bright orange. The lateral stripes are usually less well defined (may be lacking entirely), and are often less brilliant than the vertebral stripe. There is often much white showing interstitially. Dark spots may be present, and if so, are often most visible just above the lateral stripe. The belly is equally variable in color. It may be yellowish, gray, or brown, or any of numerous shades between. There are often reddish or dark spots present on the belly scutes. There are usually only 7 supralabial scales. The dorsal scales are keeled, most often in 17 rows, and the anal plate is not divided.

Similar species: Other sympatric garter snakes have a proportionately wider head, a higher number of supralabial scales, or a higher number of rows of body scales, and lack red markings on the belly.

ADDITIONAL SUBSPECIES

None.

112. Aridland Ribbon Snake
Thamnophis proximus diabolicus

Abundance/Range: This is the only ribbon snake to enter the American west, and it barely does so. While not an uncommon snake, it is normally not present in great density, either. This snake occurs in two disjunct areas, one along the Pecos Drainage in New Mexico, the other in northeastern New Mexico.

Habitat: Despite its aridland habitat, this ribbon snake (like the other races) is persistently aquatic. Although it may wander short distances from permanent and semipermanent water sources, it is most often found along rivers, streams, stock tanks, irrigation canals, golf course water hazards, and in similar habitats.

Size: This ribbon snake is adult at 20–32 inches in length. The largest authenticated specimen was 48½ inches long. The tail comprises about one third of the snake's total length. Females tend to be longer and of greater girth than males.

Identifying features: The aridland ribbon snake is typified by an ochre, buff, or orange vertebral stripe and by well-developed yellow(ish) lateral stripes on scale rows 3 and 4. The lateral stripe is bordered ventrally by a dark field. The ground color is olive gray, olive brown, or nearly black. The venter is light and unmarked. There is often a small light spot on the top of the head, just anterior to the beginning of the vertebral stripe. The head

Aridland Ribbon Snake

is narrow, but moderately distinct from the neck. The 8 supralabial scales are not barred, an important fact when identification is in question.

The scales are keeled, usually in 19 rows at midbody, and the anal plate is not divided.

Similar snakes: The lined snake has a double row of half-moons on its venter. Garter snakes are less attenuate, but can be difficult to differentiate. The Northern Mexican garter snake and the Plains garter snake have barred supralabial scales. The New Mexican garter snake and the wandering garter snake have the lateral stripe on scale rows 2 and 3. The western black-necked garter snake, the northern checkered garter snake, and the northern Mexican garter snake all have conspicuous dark neck blotches. Patch-nosed snakes and the various striped whipsnakes have smooth scales.

ADDITIONAL SUBSPECIES

Although there are none in our area, there are three additional forms in the eastern United States and two Mexican forms.

113. Plains Garter Snakes

Thamnophis radix

Abundance/Range: In certain of the better habitats, where moisture is adequate, and food in the form of worms and frogs is plentiful, *T. radix* can be an abundant species. In marginally acceptable areas the snakes may be absent or uncommon. The range of the Plains garter snake extends from south central Canada in the north southward in a broad swath to northern Texas and northern New Mexico. There are two disjunct populations in Ohio and southern Illinois.

Habitat: Although often referred to as a species of the wet central prairies, the Plains garter snake occurs in a vast array of habitats. It is found in backyards and wet mountain meadows, in drainage ditches and at marsh edge, and in sloughs and the environs of ponds. It does wander from the immediate proximity of water during wet weather, but is less prone to stray far afield during dry periods.

Size: This is a relatively large and heavy-bodied garter snake. Adults can attain 3½ feet. However, the more normal size is 18–28 inches. Females are often the larger sex.

Identifying features: This snake may be quite pretty or quite drab, but is usually in between. The ground color varies from olive brown to black to a rather brownish red. No matter the ground color, the snake has a well-developed vertebral stripe that is orange(ish) anteriorly, shading to yellow posteriorly. The lateral stripes are more poorly defined than the vertebral stripe and occupy the 3rd and 4th scale rows above the ventral scutes. Except on the black or nearly black specimens, a dark checkerboarding is also very visible in the dorsolateral dark field. A row of dark spots is usually present below the light lateral lines. There are a pair of large dark neck blotches (but these are not as conspicuous as in the black-necked, checkered, and northern Mexican garter snakes). The supralabial scales are vertically barred with dark pigment. The Plains garter snake may have 19 or 21 rows of keeled dorsal scales, and has a single anal scale. It has a

Plains Garter Snake

particularly long activity pattern, emerging from hibernation very early in the spring and being among the last species to enter hibernation.

Similar snakes: The various striped whipsnakes and patch-nosed snakes lack checkers and have smooth scales. Terrestrial and common garter snakes have the stripes on the 2nd and 3rd scale rows.

ADDITIONAL SUBSPECIES

There are currently no recognized subspecies.

114. Narrow-headed Garter Snake
Thamnophis rufipunctatus

Abundance/Range: This distinctive garter snake is becoming increasingly rare and is protected by law in Arizona and New Mexico. The range of this snake in the United States is a rather narrow swath that extends eastward from eastern central Arizona to western central New Mexico. It is more widely distributed in central northern Mexico.

Habitat: Look for this garter snake in rocky stretches of streams and in lakeside rock piles. It is almost always found in areas where cover is readily available.

Narrow-headed Garter Snake

Size: This is a medium-sized garter snake. Most seen are between 16 and 26 inches in length, and the maximum recorded length is only 34 inches.

Identifying features: The narrow-headed garter snake looks and acts more like a water snake than a garter snake. Rather than being prominently striped (if stripes are present at all, they are weakly defined and only on the sides of the neck) this snake is prominently spotted. The ground color varies from a dingy olive to a reddish brown. The pattern consists of narrow, dark middorsal blotches and alternating dark lateral spots. It is dusky ventrally, but lightest on the throat and neck. The eyes are situated high on the sides of the rather narrow head. The colors and patterns blend remarkably well with the rocks, soil and vegetation of its streamside habitats. The keeled dorsal scales are in 21 rows and the anal plate is usually single (divided in about 10% of the snakes found).

Similar snakes: In appearance, this snake is as dissimilar to other garter snakes as it is to other snakes in other genera. It is often thought to be a water snake but is not apt to be mistaken for any other species in its range.

ADDITIONAL SUBSPECIES

None.

COMMON GARTER SNAKES

115. Red-spotted Garter Snake
Thamnophis sirtalis concinnus

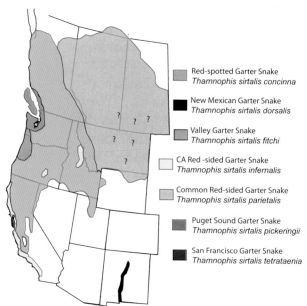

Red-spotted Garter Snake
Thamnophis sirtalis concinna

New Mexican Garter Snake
Thamnophis sirtalis dorsalis

Valley Garter Snake
Thamnophis sirtalis fitchi

CA Red -sided Garter Snake
Thamnophis sirtalis infernalis

Common Red-sided Garter Snake
Thamnophis sirtalis parietalis

Puget Sound Garter Snake
Thamnophis sirtalis pickeringii

San Francisco Garter Snake
Thamnophis sirtalis tetrataenia

Abundance/Range: This remains one of the more commonly encountered snakes within its range. This Pacific Coast sub-species ranges northward from western central Oregon to extreme southwestern Washington.

Habitat: This snake may be encountered in a variety of habitats, ranging from woodlands to open damp meadows and rocky, open hillsides.

Size: This snake is adult at between 16 and 28 inches in length, and seldom exceeds 36 inches.

Identifying features: Like many garter snakes, this race is variable in coloration, but all are beautiful. Many have a ground color of ebony, with highlights of vermilion and lemon. The brilliant yellow vertebral stripe is well-defined; the lateral stripes are poorly defined or lacking. The lower sides are patterned with regularly spaced, bright red spots. The top of the head is orange red. The eyes are proportionately large. There are usually 7 upper labial scales and 10 lower labials.

Some specimens are much paler (lacking much or all of the red), being ebony and butter yellow instead.

The venter is bluish to blue green along the midline, and darker along the sides. The throat is paler than the belly. There are usually 19 rows of keeled scales at midbody; the anal plate is not divided.

Red-spotted Garter Snake

Similar snakes: Use range maps to assist in identification of all garter snakes. For descriptions of other races of the common garter snake, please read accounts 115 through 121. The wandering garter snake usually has 8 upper labial scales; the northwestern garter snake usually has 7 upper labials. Both have proportionately smaller eyes than the red-spotted (or other) race(s) of the common garter snake. Both the wandering and the northwestern garter snakes lack well defined red spots on the sides.

ADDITIONAL SUBSPECIES

In one or another of its 12 subspecies, the common garter snake is found from America's Atlantic coast to the Pacific, and from southern Canada to the southernmost tip of the Florida Peninsula to just a few miles north of the USA/Mexican border in California. The common garter snake is, however, absent from the American southwest, where it is replaced by aridland adapted species. The common garter snake is also absent from a vast area of northern Montana, southern Saskatchewan, and southern Alberta. Over most of that area it is replaced by the Plains, *T. radix*, and wandering, *T. elegans vagrans*, garter snakes.

It is in the western United States that the most strikingly colored subspecies of the common garter snake are found.

New Mexican Garter Snake

116. The New Mexican Garter Snake, *T. s. dorsalis*, is largely restricted to the Rio Grande Valley of New Mexico, but one disjunct population also occurs in the Pecos River Valley of that state and two additional populations exist in western Chihuahua, Mexico. This race often has red on the sides, but the red may be largely (or entirely) restricted to interstitial (between the scales) areas. The red is often quite dark, and does not contrast greatly with the black ground color. The vertebral and lateral stripes are very prominent and of a pretty butter yellow.

117. The Valley Garter Snake, *T. s. fitchi*, is also a dark-colored race. It has a variable amount of the red on the sides but both the yellow lateral and middorsal stripes are prominent. A gray morph exists in the vicinity of Crater Lake, Oregon. The valley garter snake occurs from extreme southern Alaska (the only snake to be found in that state) through British Columbia, Idaho, and southward into Utah and Nevada, and from there westward to northern and central California and eastern Oregon and Washington.

Valley Garter Snake

118. The California Red-sided Garter Snake, *T. s. infernalis*, is another of the very pretty westerners. It is found over much of coastal California. This latter race looks very much like the prairie red-sided garter snake (from which it is geographically widely separated) but has poorly defined lateral stripes and a red or orange(ish) head.

California Red-sided Garter Snake

Prairie Red-sided Garter Snake

119. The Prairie Red-sided Garter Snake, *T. s. parietalis*, is another variably colored race. Typically this common Plains states and northwestern garter snake has discrete red bars extending upward from the well-defined lateral stripe, well into the black of the sides. Some specimens have the red extending in checkerboard-like squares from lateral to dorsal stripe. Other specimens may lack much of the red. The head of this race is black. This creature gathers in incredibly high numbers for hibernation and for breeding (much of which is accomplished, both in autumn and spring, at the winter denning sites).

120. The Puget Sound Garter Snake, *T. s. pickeringii*, is found to the north of the range of the red-spotted garter in northwestern Washington and southwestern British Columbia (including Vancouver Island). This is primarily a black snake with rather well defined white or pale yellow vertebral and lateral stripes. If red is present, it is dull, narrow, and often only interstitial. The top of the head is dark.

121. The San Francisco Garter Snake, *T. s. tetrataenia*, occurs in reduced numbers in its ever-dwindling habitat on the western San Francisco peninsula of central California. This is one of the world's most beautiful snakes. It is federally endangered and is entirely protected. The San Fran-

Puget Sound Garter Snake

cisco garter snake is typified by a solid fire orange to red orange dorso-lateral stripe along each side and a well-defined vertebral stripe of pale to greenish yellow. The lateral stripes are usually less intensely colored than the vertebral stripe. The belly is bluish green.

San Francisco Garter Snake

Lined Snake, Genus *Tropidoclonion*

In gross appearance, the lined snake is much like a small garter snake and is, indeed, very closely allied to the snakes of the genus *Thamnophis*. From them, it may be immediately told by the presence of the double row of bold half-moons extending from the neck, virtually to the tailtip along the belly.

Lined snakes are reluctant to bite; their saliva composition is unknown. The lined snake is an earthworm specialist. Although some insects and sowbugs have been mentioned as dietary components, it is invariably earthworms that arouse the most interest of the snakes.

This prairieland snake produces living young. Neonates are 4½–5 inches in length. The largest documented clutch contained 17 babies.

The 19 rows of scales are keeled; the anal plate is undivided.

122. Lined Snake

Tropidoclonion lineatum

Abundance/Range: Because of its need for moist habitats, the lined snake is found in localized noncontiguous populations throughout most of its range. It may be moderately uncommon in some areas, abundant in others, and completely absent from still others. Because of its secretive habits, it is a difficult species to accurately census. The principal range of the lined snake is east of our coverage area. However, several disjunct populations are found in southern and central New Mexico and eastern Colorado.

Habitat: There could hardly be a more adaptable snake than this species. Principally a species of the open grasslands, the lined snake has adapted well to the habitat degradation of humans, continuing to exist in gardens, parks, the environs of drainage ditches, dumps, and many similar moisture-retaining habitats. The lined snake is particularly active following warm rains. Because it is so secretive, it is very easy to overlook fairly sizable populations of this small snake. The lined snake not only utilizes even the smallest pieces of human-generated debris, but also secretes it-

Lined Snake

self beneath plant material, rocks, and other such natural surface cover. The lined snake is an accomplished burrower.

Size: Normally lined snakes measure between 8 and 12 inches in length when adult. A specimen of 15 inches is considered huge, and the record size of 22 inches is Brobdingnagian!

Identifying features: Some examples of this little snake look like a cross between a dwarfed garter snake and a brown snake. The dorsal coloration is a warm brown to an olive brown. This is divided by a whitish or tan vertebral stripe peppered along its outer edges with tiny dark markings. The dark dorsal color may be bordered ventrally by a narrow dark line, which is then bordered on scale rows 2 and 3 by a whitish line. The dark line separating the dorsal ground color from the light lateral stripe may be absent. The belly is whitish to yellowish, but is patterned for its length by a double row of small dark half-moons.

Similar species: The double row of ventral half-moons will identify the lined snake.

ADDITIONAL SUBSPECIES

None.

7

Coral Snakes, Family Elapidae

This family contains the deadly cobras, mambas, kraits, and their allies, which all have fixed (unmovable) front fangs. Most of the family is of primarily Old World distribution, with only one member, the micrurine elapines (the coral snakes), found in the New World. Only a single species, the small Arizona coral snake, occurs in western North America north of Mexico. It is clad in rings of red, yellow, and black.

A ditty, red to yellow, kill a fellow, red to black, venom lack, is often used to remember the color sequence that identifies this coral snake. However, if you are having difficulty remembering the rhyme, simply think of a traffic signal. On this familiar icon the two caution colors, red and yellow, touch, as they do on the coral snake.

Arizona Coral Snake

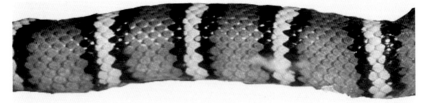

Mountain Kingsnakes and Milk Snakes

This snake has a reputation for being a reluctant biter, and is often handled with relative impunity. However, like many members of the cobra family, it has an unpredictable disposition and it may bite at any time. It should be considered a very dangerous snake and never lifted or restrained by hand. Despite the erroneous belief that this snake can bite only small extremities, it is capable of biting almost any exposed body part. A bite should receive immediate medical attention. The venom is predominantly neurotoxic.

Coral snakes eat small reptiles—mostly smooth-scaled snakes, with a strong preference for blind snakes of the genus *Leptotyphlops*. Black-headed snakes, night snakes, and small skinks are also occasionally eaten.

The Arizona coral snake is oviparous. Clutches are small, consisting of 1–3 relatively large, elongate eggs. In Arizona, eggs are laid during the summer months, apparently in conjunction with the monsoon season. Depending on soil temperature and moisture, the incubation duration seems to last for 55–65 days. Hatchlings are about 7½ inches in length.

Candy Canes with a Punch

While on our way into Sonora, Mexico, Brad Smith and I had made a pit stop in a remote area of south central Arizona. The sun was sinking rapidly, setting the western sky aflame. A desert tortoise crossed the road, stopping at the edge to eat some very unpalatable-looking grasses. We photographed the tortoise, then resumed the drive. We were soon on a rocky stretch of road.

"Snake!" Brad screamed. Having seen nothing, I slammed on the brakes and hoped for the best. Brad was out before the car had stopped. Dancing around in midroad, Brad excitedly exclaimed, "It's a coral snake!" It was Brad's first field sighting of the Arizona coral snake, *Micruroides e. euryxanthus*. The snake had no intention of allowing us to deter it from its journey. It had just come out of a heavy patch of grasses and cacti and was determined to quickly enter similar habitat on the far side of the road. There were no other vehicles on the road, so we decided to try to photograph the little creature. It moved. We followed. It moved more. We followed again. It went beneath a rock and didn't emerge. We waited. We finally had the cameras ready and I flipped the rock. The little red, white, and black snake lay coiled with its head hidden. I touched it and it started, then stopped, head exposed. Pictures were taken and the three of us—the snake, Brad, and I—continued on our journeys. We were far more excited about our find than the snake had been about being found.

continued

Despite their small size, these little cobra allies have functional fangs and a virulent venom. You need only witness the speed with which the venom overpowers the coral snake's lizard or snake prey to realize that this is not a species you would wish to be bitten by. Treat them with the care and respect they deserve.

123. Arizona Coral Snake

Micruroides euryxanthus euryxanthus

Abundance/Range: Because of its secretive habits, the Arizona coral snake continues to persist even in suburban areas. It ranges westward from extreme southwestern New Mexico to central Arizona. It also may be found south of our border to central Sonora, Mexico. It is not uncommon, but is seldom seen.

Habitat: This small and beautiful snake occurs in myriad habitats in Arizona. It may occasionally be encountered in manicured, irrigated yards, crossing suburban roadways (especially following a substantial rain), traversing unpopulated deserts, or on rock-strewn plains and meadows. This snake is also seen on mesquite flats in river valleys. It may seek seclusion beneath rocks and other surface debris, but is also an accomplished burrower. Upper elevational limit for this species is about 5,800 feet.

Size: Most specimens of this snake are 15 inches or less in length. Maximum size is thought to be 21 inches.

Identifying features: The Arizona coral snake is of slender build and colored in what Americans have come to think of as the characteristic coral snake colors and pattern. Broad rings of black, red, and yellow, with red and yellow touching, encircle the body. We hasten to mention that neither this pattern nor the colors hold true on many Neotropical coral snakes.

The coral snake has a narrow head with a black snout that it may flatten when frightened. The snout is bluntly rounded. A loreal scale is lacking. The tail, ringed in black and yellow, is quite blunt. The shiny nonkeeled scales are in 15 rows at midbody. The anal plate is divided.

Arizona Coral Snake

Similar species: The various tricolored king and milk snakes have the two caution colors separated by bands of black. The banded phase of the ground snake lacks yellow bands. Both the shovel-nosed snake and the banded sand snake are saddled, not ringed, and have immaculate cream-colored bellies.

Comments: The Arizona coral snake is nervous and "twitchy" when frightened or touched. It often hides its head beneath its body coils when startled. A frightened snake may also curl and elevate its tailtip, waving it to and fro, perhaps to decoy attention from its head. The Arizona coral snake may display cloacal popping, everting and withdrawing the vent lining. This makes a characteristic popping sound.

ADDITIONAL SUBSPECIES

None in the United States.

8

Sea Snakes, Family Hydrophiidae

Despite being assigned to a separate family, the sea snakes are essentially oceangoing cobras. Many genera and many more species are present in the tropical oceans of the world. Only a single species, the pelagic yellow-bellied sea snake, *Pelamis platurus,* enters our waters, and then only by accident.

All sea snakes have fixed (immovable) front fangs, and all are dangerously toxic. Most are reluctant to bite unless carelessly restrained. Some apparently display increased aggression during the breeding season. All eat fish; some specialize in eels; a few consume fish eggs. It seems unlikely that venom is expended during a fish-egg repast.

Sea snakes have flattened, oarlike tails and swim with a typical side to side undulation. They lack enlarged belly scutes. Many are rather helpless when out of the water. Both egg-laying and live-bearing species are known.

Little is known about the breeding biology of the yellow-bellied sea snake. Pairs have been found knotted together and what have been thought

to be breeding congregations have been seen. Breeding may occur only in the parts of its range where mean water temperatures attain or exceed 68°F. *Pelamis* is a live-bearing sea snake. In coastal Central America, 1–6 neonates are produced. Neonates are between 8 and 10 inches in length.

Pelagic Paddle-tails

We were sitting in a little open boat a mile or so off the central Pacific coast of Costa Rica. A small turtle (probably an olive ridley, but not confirmed) swam beneath us. It was a hot, sunny day with a breeze barely stirring. We motored from slick to slick hoping we would see the only documented sea snake of the Americas, the pelagic yellow-bellied sea snake, *Pelamis platurus*. A friend wielding long forceps hung anxiously over the bow of the small vessel. He was hoping to collect the snakes for a proposed display at an American zoo.

"Isquierda, isquierda"—and the motor man swerved us to the left. The forceps entered the water and were withdrawn holding a squirming and biting 2-foot-long sea snake. For another hour or two we stayed asea, putt-putting slowly from slick to slick, and when time was finally called, about a dozen sea snakes swam in the deep buckets brought for the purpose. All were black and yellow, but there the similarity stopped. The amount of yellow and pattern—especially the pattern on the flattened paddlelike tail—varied greatly from snake to snake.

Soon we were back ashore with the beautiful animals.

A subsequent walk along the rocky shoreline disclosed a few more sea snakes and emphasized how specialized this snake actually is. Having evolved for a life at sea, the snakes are very poorly adapted for movement when on the shore. In fact, their ability to move is so limited that most quickly gave up the effort, merely lying quietly in ophidian hope that the next wave would carry them back into the water. Some would be lucky, but from the carcasses we found it was obvious that some were not.

As we left the seashore we fully realized how lucky we'd been to succeed on our first effort. It often takes numerous lengthy searches to find even one of these snakes, and we'd found more than a dozen. This sea snake has occasionally been recorded along the shoreline of southern California, where it is very rare, but it does occur more commonly in Hawaiian waters.

124. Yellow-bellied Sea Snake
Pelamis platurus

Abundance/Range: This snake is one of the most common and widely distributed snakes in the world. It is known from most areas of the Indian and Pacific oceans (including Hawaiian waters), and can be common along the Pacific coasts of most Central American countries. It occurs also along Mexico's Pacific coast (including the Baja Peninsula) and is considered an accidental occurrence in American waters, where it has been found on the California coast as far north as southern Orange County.

Habitat: This fully aquatic snake is entirely at home in warm ocean waters, and just as entirely out of its element when washed ashore. Movement on land is all but impossible. This snake most often occurs under floating debris in the quiet slicks that are formed by converging ocean currents. It is alert, and may dive deeply at the approach of a boat.

Size: Although most specimens seen in the eastern Pacific are in the 18–25-inch size range, in Australian waters specimens of slightly more than 3½ feet in total length have been found.

Identifying features: The yellow-bellied sea snake is aptly named. It is a very dark brown to black dorsally, has bright yellow lower sides, and

Yellow-bellied Sea Snake

is often an equally bright yellow below. In some cases, the midventral area may be olive yellow. The amount of yellow may vary. In Costa Rican waters we found a snake of this species that had only a narrow vertebral stripe of black; the remainder of the snake was bright yellow. Solid yellow examples have been noted. The delineation of the two colors is precise. The flattened, oarlike yellow tail bears a variable black pattern. It may be barred, spotted, and/or scalloped. The snout is long and the head is distinctly triangular both in profile and when viewed from above. The gape is wider. Both the eyes and nostrils of the yellow-bellied sea snake are set high on the sides of the head. The nostrils are valvular and can be closed when the snake dives. The scales are nonimbricate (do not overlap) and, although nonkeeled, are rough to the touch. Neonates are similar to the adults in color and pattern.

Similar species: None in American waters.

Comments: Although most commonly seen after it has been washed ashore, this snake drifts far and wide with the ocean currents.

Ecdysis (shedding) is facilitated by the snake forming one or more knots in its body and crawling through these. The roughened scales assist in removing the skin. It is thought that crawling through the tightly knotted body also removes ectoparasites such as barnacles.

ADDITIONAL SUBSPECIES

None.

9

Vipers

Pit Vipers, Family Viperidae

RATTLESNAKES, SUBFAMILY CROTALINAE

The rattlesnakes are pit vipers. This name is derived from the presence of a heat (infrared) sensory pit on each side of their face. The pit permits these snakes to home in on warm-blooded prey (such as mice, rats, squirrels, and rabbits) and to strike, delivering a venomous bite, unerringly, even in complete darkness.

The pit vipers have a long hollow fang attached to a rotatable maxillary bone on each side of the upper jaw. The maxilla can be rotated posteriorly to fold the fangs against the roof of the mouth when the mouth is closed, or rotated anteriorly to direct the fangs almost straight forward when the snake is indulging in a gaping, lunging, forward strike. If a fang breaks, it is quickly replaced. The fangs are ducted to venom glands at the rear of the head. It is these glands, and the controlling muscles that surround them, that cause the posterior enlargement so typical of the head of the viperine snakes. A pit viper can regulate the amount of venom expended during a bite. Many bites are "dry"; no venom is injected during the strike. During other bites a full complement of venom is injected. Secondary infections can be caused by any bite; a creature that eats carrion as well as freshly killed prey does not have a clean mouth.

The venom, a complex combination of enzymes and other proteins, has been developed primarily for food procurement and secondarily as a defense mechanism. The drop for drop toxicity of pit viper venom varies species by species, and even within a species. The venom of most North American rattlesnakes is primarily hemorrhagic, but that of some is strongly neurotoxic.

The Cascabels—Snakes with a Rattle

In the American west, *not* stumbling across a rattlesnake of some species while afield is often more difficult than finding one. It seems that rattlers of one species or another and sometimes several species are wherever a field researcher treads. Prairieland or desert, lowlands or montane fast-nesses, amid human habitation or in remote rangelands—all of these and others are habitats to "buzztails."

Some of the rattlers are confusingly similar; others are of such distinct appearance that they can be mistaken for no other snake species. Some are irascible to the point of actual feistiness, calling attention to themselves with their incessant buzzing when they would have been otherwise unnoticed. Others cannot be induced to rattle, hiding their head amid silent coils if prodded.

There are two genera of rattlesnakes in our west. One, the genus *Sistrurus*, is represented by a single species, but there are eleven species of typical rattlesnakes of the genus *Crotalus*.

Working our way westward, Patti and I had already happened across the very common western diamond-backed rattler and the look-alike Mojave rattler. In the foothills of Arizona's Sky Islands we had seen northern black-tailed rattlers. Now we were ascending a walking trail in Ramsey Canyon in the Huachuca Mountains of southeastern Arizona. Our quest was the Arizona ridge-nosed rattlesnake, a beautiful, locally

continued

distributed, diminutive species clad in the hues of dead grasses and leaves and of rocks.

The trail took us upward from the headquarters, past a pond rimmed with leopard frogs, through rocky oak woodland, along boulder-strewn canyons, parallel to an intermittent stream, and eventually through pine-woods. Nuthatches and chickadees stared curiously at us. We passed a twin-spotted rattlesnake atop a creviced boulder. Banded rock rattlers basked placidly on sun-drenched escarpments. Mountain spiny lizards were abundantly evident.

More oaks, scattered sparsely through and around verdant mountain meadows. Almost at trail edge a little reddish brown rattler sat amid some fallen leaves. The most visible markings were its vivid white facial stripes, and it was these that had caught out attention as the snake turned its head slightly to watch our approach. An Arizona ridge-nose! Mission accomplished.

Typical Rattlesnakes, Genus *Crotalus*

These snakes are of New World distribution. In the west, rattlesnakes of one or more species range southward from the southernmost regions of the western Canadian provinces to the Mexican border, then beyond to Argentina.

The rattlesnakes of the genus *Crotalus* have finely fragmented crown scales. This alone will allow easy differentiation from the rattlers in the genus *Sistrurus* which, like most harmless snakes, have 9 large plates on the top of their head. For rattlesnakes, the body scales are keeled and the ventral scale is not divided.

Rattlesnakes are wait-and-ambush hunters that, by chemosensory testing, are able to unerringly position themselves along active rodent trails. Most strike and immediately release their prey, allowing the venom a chance to immobilize the stricken animal before trailing it. It has been shown that rattlesnakes are able to differentiate between the trail of a non-envenomated animal and an envenomated one, even if of the same species.

Many species of rattlesnakes are only subtly different from each other. Such things as uneven versus smooth edges of supraocular scales, or the number of internasal scales in contact with the rostral scale, are identifying criteria. We hasten to advise that close-focusing binoculars will help keep you a safe distance from a venomous snake while allowing you to see salient identifying points. If you are close enough to a living specimen to see many of these characteristic differences with a naked eye, you are much too close for your safety. The location and habitat in which the snake is seen will also help with identification.

When fully adult, male rattlesnakes are often larger than the females of their species.

The males of many species are known to indulge in stylized "combat rituals" or fights. These occur most often during the breeding season, and usually involve reproductively ready males. In this, the males approach each other and, pressing venter against venter, elevate the anterior of their body until the head is high above the ground. Eventually they may entwine necks and forebodies, and the heavier snake will topple and dominate the lighter one. No biting occurs during these bouts; after sustaining several body slams, the subordinate male will usually disengage from the combat and leave the scene.

It has been found that the females of at least some rattlesnake species (black-tails and prairie rattlers among them) remain with their young for about 10 days after birth. The gravid females of many species move only short distances. This is especially true when parturition is imminent.

Rattlesnakes have vertically elliptical pupils that dilate widely in the dark.

The rattle is present at birth as a single segment button. A basal segment is added at each shed. It is not until at least two segments are present that the rattle can produce the characteristic whirring sound.

Rattlesnakes give birth to live young. Because of the variability in size and number, statistics on the neonates will be mentioned in the individual species accounts.

125. Western Diamond-backed Rattlesnake

Crotalus atrox

Abundance/Range: Despite decades of persecution at the hands of humans, including the barbaric practice of rattlesnake roundups, the western diamond-back remains abundant over most, if not all of its range. Although it may be absent from many urban areas, it continues to persist

in suburban habitats and may follow canals, ditches, and riverbeds well into rather heavily populated areas. Babies may be seen in late summer and early autumn, often by the dozens, as they seek secure areas in which to overwinter.

This rattlesnake ranges westward and southward from central Arkansas to southeastern California and central Mexico.

Habitat: This is one of the most ubiquitous of arid- and semiarid-land rattlesnakes. It occurs in sparsely vegetated desert and ranchland, in chaparral, on rocky plains, and in lushly grassed lomas, as well as in all areas between, and is the rattlesnake most commonly seen in suburban areas and crossing roadways in the evening. It has been found from sea level to elevations of 8,200 feet.

Size: The western diamond-back is the largest of the western rattlers, and second only to the eastern diamond-back in size. Although those seen are often 1–4 feet in length, specimens of 5 feet or more are still seen with regularity. The record size is 7½ feet! Neonates vary from as small as 8½ inches to about 13 inches in length.

Identifying features: The western diamond-backed rattlesnake is variable both in ground color and in pattern intensity. Typically the diamond

Western Diamond-backed Rattlesnake

Western Diamond-backed Rattlesnake

pattern appears faded or dusty but is still very apparent. Conversely, on some examples the pattern is pale and difficult to discern. The diamonds are outlined in shades of gray (often ash), bordered on the inside by light to very dark brown. The ground color usually blends well with the soils on which this snake is found. The ground color may vary from pale gray through dark gray, to a deep red. The face has a prominent light diagonal preocular bar and a somewhat less prominent diagonal postocular bar. The posterior stripe touches the jawline well anterior to the rear of the mouth (binoculars will help immeasurably in ascertaining the stripe position!). The tail is prominently patterned with black and white (or light gray) rings of roughly equal width. Some rings may be broken and offset middorsally. Because males have a longer tail, they often have a higher ring count, but this is far from an infallible method of determining sex. The scales are keeled, in 23–25 rows, and the anal plate is not divided.

Similar species: The red diamond rattlesnake has a similar appearance but has scales in 29 rows, is redder than most diamond-backs, and occurs in the United States only in southwestern California. The Mojave rattlesnake is also rather similar, but has tail rings of uneven width and often broken. The ground color is often gray green and the dorsal pattern is usually stronger than that of the western diamond-back. Additionally, the posterior facial stripe of the Mojave rattler either touches the corner of the mouth or passes behind it. The Mojave also has enlarged scales between the eyes (again, these are visible with binoculars). Other rattlesnake species are either prominently speckled, have bars rather than dorsal diamonds, or have the dorsal markings widely separated.

Comments: This rattlesnake is often defensive but less often aggressive. It has a long strike, dangerously toxic venom, and should be given a wide berth.

When provoked this snake will often stand its ground, neck raised high in an effective striking coil, head slightly lowered, rattling loudly. In fact, many specimens would remain unseen were it not for their tendency to loudly rattle at the slightest disturbance.

Clutches contain 4–25 babies. It is probable that most females breed biennially, but some may reproduce only every third year. Males indulge in ritualistic combat (shoving and body pinning) that may be associated with the breeding biology or territoriality.

ADDITIONAL SUBSPECIES

None.

126. Mojave Desert Sidewinder

Crotalus cerastes cerastes

Mojave Desert Sidewinder
Crotalus cerastes cerastes

Sonoran Sidewinder
Crotalus c. cercobombus

Colorado Desert Sidewinder
Crotalus c. laterorepens

Abundance/Range: This is a common rattlesnake. It is secretive and primarily nocturnal, hence easily overlooked. This is the northernmost of the three subspecies of sidewinder. It occurs in desert regions from extreme southwestern Utah to eastern central California and southward to western central Arizona and adjacent California.

Habitat: Although it is typically associated with areas of fine, shifting, wind-blown sands, the sidewinder also inhabits desert areas with somewhat more stable soil characteristics. It seems particularly common in areas vegetated by creosote bushes and may often be found near kangaroo rat warrens. This snake has been encountered at up to 6,000 feet in elevation.

Mojave Desert Sidewinder

Size: Although most specimens seen are 12–18 inches in length, sidewinders are known to attain an overall length of 33 inches. Neonates are about 7 inches in length at birth.

Identifying features: There are few snake species that blend better with their backgrounds than the sidewinder. Light-colored specimens are usually associated with light-colored soils, while darker specimens often occur in regions of darker soil. The ground color of this subspecies is often darkest middorsally. There are about 40 lighter middorsal blotches, well defined on their leading and trailing edges, but often blending almost imperceptibly with the ground color laterally. The light blotches are often wider than the dark interspaces. There is usually a pair of dark spots on the rear of the head. A dark, diagonal facial bar is present. The diagnostic supraocular horns are a feature shared only with the other two races of sidewinder. The Mojave sidewinder has keeled body scales in 21 rows and the basal segment of the rattle is brown. The anal plate is not divided.

Similar species: There are several rattlesnakes of similar coloration, but only the sidewinder has supraorbital horns. In northern Baja, the Baja California rattlesnake, *Crotalus enyo*, may be encountered. Although the supraocular scales of this latter species are tipped upward, they do not form horns.

Comments: The three subspecies of sidewinder are poorly differentiated. Use range as a primary criterion for determining the subspecies. The sidewinder is often referred to as the horned rattlesnake.

Relatively long fangs, a potent venom, and a readiness to bite if molested dictate that this rattlesnake should not be closely approached.

The curious "sidewinding," the throwing of raised body loops to the side, is a mode of locomotion used by no other rattlesnake of the United States. The sidewinder is a wait-and-ambush species. The snake buries itself just beneath the surface of the desert sand, often in the proximity of kangaroo rat warrens, but sometimes along pocket mouse or lizard trails. In such a position, often with only the top of its head visible, the snake is easily overlooked by both prey and humans. The sidewinder is feared by some humans, and summarily dispatched whenever seen.

It is not known with certainty whether the sidewinder is an annual or biennial breeder. From 2 to 18 live babies are produced from late summer to mid-autumn. The usual number of young varies between 4 and 10.

ADDITIONAL SUBSPECIES

127. The Sonoran Sidewinder, *C. c. cercobombus,* ranges over much of arid south central Arizona and northwestern mainland Mexico. This subspecies of the sidewinder is often quite red in color. The (approximately) 40 light dorsal blotches are often poorly defined and usually narrower than

Sonoran Sidewinder

the areas of ground color that separate them. There are 21 rows of scales and a black basal rattle segment.

128. The Colorado Desert Sidewinder, *C. c. laterorepens*, occurs in south-eastern California, southwestern Arizona, northwestern Sonora, and east-ern Baja California Norte. It is a pallid race on which the 40 (plus or mi-nus a few) pale dorsal blotches are often wider than the dark interspaces. The scales are in 23 rows, and the basal rattle segment is black; it is often brown(ish) on immature specimens.

Colorado Desert Sidewinder

129. Mottled Rock Rattlesnake
Crotalus lepidus lepidus

Abundance/Range: This is a moderately common rattlesnake. In the United States, the mottled rock rattlesnake is largely restricted to western Texas, from the Edwards Plateau to Hudspeth County. In our area it occurs in Eddy and adjacent Otero coun-ties, New Mexico. It ranges southward to the vicinity of San Luis Potosi, Mexico.

Habitat: This rattler is a denizen of rocky mountain sides, cliff faces, escarpments and outcroppings, and

Mottled Rock Rattlesnake
Crotalus lepidus lepidus

Banded Rock Rattlesnake
Crotalus l. klauberi

Mottled Rock Rattlesnake

fissured canyon walls. This snake prefers elevations between 1,000 and 9,500 feet.

Size: The normal size range of this small rattlesnake is 12–18 inches. The record size is just over 30 inches. Neonates are about 7 inches in total length.

Identifying features: Despite having a relatively small range, the mottled rock rattlesnake is quite variable in color. The ground color typically blends well with the color of the rocks among which the snake is found. These snakes can vary from pinkish, to russet, gray, bluish gray, olive brown, to a chalky white (and all colors between these). The primary bands are usually at least faintly visible (sometimes vividly so), and the secondary mottling is somewhat less contrasting. This snake is capable of quite considerable day to night color changes. The top of the head is weakly mottled or plain. A diagonal dark bar is present from beneath each eye to the corner of the mouth. The weakly banded tail is a rather bright yellow to orange at birth, but darkens somewhat as the snake ages. The keeled body scales are arranged in 23 rows. The anal plate is not divided.

Similar species: Only the closely related banded rock rattlesnake (account 130) might be confused with the mottled rock rattler.

Comments: This rattler is not often encountered crossing roadways; however, it may wander well away from its typical habitat on hot summer nights following an afternoon shower.

This is a feisty little rattler that is quick to buzz if disturbed, quick to bite if restrained, and quick to seek seclusion in horizontal fissures or among jumbles of rocks if approached. It often continues to rattle long after it has retreated out of sight to safety. When cool, the mottled rock rattlesnake often thermoregulates from the comparative safety of a fissure by extending a body coil out into the warming sunlight. As its body temperature nears optimum, more and more of the coil is drawn back into the shade. This little snake is active principally by day, but when temperatures become very hot it may remain active until long after nightfall.

It seems probable that the mottled rock rattlesnake is a biennial breeder. Clutches contain 1–8 neonates, with the usual number being 2–4.

ADDITIONAL SUBSPECIES

130. The Banded Rock Rattlesnake, *C. l. klauberi* is the more westerly subspecies. It ranges westward from the Franklin Mountains of west Texas to several of the mountain ranges of southeastern Arizona, and southward to Jalisco, Mexico. Like the mottled rock rattler, the banded race is always

Banded Rock Rattlesnake

Banded Rock Rattle-
snake

associated with rocky habitats. It may be found in rocky, isolated canyons and mountain fastnesses, on rocky hillsides and outcroppings, and near rocky intermittent streams and rivers. The banded rock rattlesnake basks by day, but often hunts and seeks new territory at dusk or after darkness. The banded rock rattlesnake has a cleaner, less busy pattern than the more easterly mottled rock rattlesnake. In fact, many examples of the banded rock rattlesnake lack even vestiges of secondary markings between the primary bands. In many populations there is a tendency toward sexual dimorphism, with many males having a ground color of green (moss green to bluish green) while that of the females is grayish to bluish. The bands are deep brown to black. This race either has no facial markings or, if present, they are faded. The tailtip of hatchlings is bright yellow to yellow orange. This fades, but is often not entirely lost, as the snakes mature.

Several other species might be confused with the banded rock rattlesnake. Among these are the twin-spotted rattlesnake, the speckled rattlesnake, and the desert massauga. The twin-spotted rattlesnake is restricted to a few mountain tops in southeastern Arizona (and then southward into Mexico). It is grayish to brownish with twinned dorsal spots and a prominently banded tail. The massasauga prefers grassland habitats, and it has 9 large scales and prominent dark bars on the top of its head. The speckled rattlesnake occurs far to the west of the mottled rock rattler.

131. Northern Black-tailed Rattlesnake

Crotalus molossus molossus

Abundance/Range: This is a relatively common but secretive rattlesnake. The range of the black-tailed rattlesnake extends westward from Texas' Edwards Plateau to western Arizona and from southern Sonora to northern Arizona and northwestern New Mexico.

Habitat: In the minds of many, the presence of a black-tailed rattlesnake epitomizes open country, and rugged open country at that. It is a rattlesnake of rocky canyons and mountains, of talus and lava beds, of desert arroyos, rocky plains, and floodplains. It has been found in arid dunelands, in boulder-strewn flatlands, in creosote-opuntia desertlands, and in coniferous and mixed woodlands at elevations of up to 9,600 feet. It is a habitat generalist, yet a monument to the now rapidly

Northern Black-tailed Rattlesnake

Northern Black-tailed Rattlesnake, Harquahala Mountain variant

developing deserts that were considered wastelands in the days of yore. It is the rattlesnake of the western states that is more apt than other species to ascend into trees and shrubs to forage and bask.

Size: Although occasional specimens may attain just over 4½ feet in length, most specimens seen are 1½–3½ feet long. The 3–8 neonates are about 10½ inches in total length.

Identifying features: The black-tailed rattlesnake shows a considerable east to west color change. In Texas and eastern New Mexico the ground color varies from greenish brown to silvery green. The dorsal color is alternating black and silver or silver gray blotches that become less contrasting and more poorly defined posteriorly. The neck tends to bear paired black stripes. The black dorsal blotches, variable and uneven in outline, usually contain light centers (that may break the dark blotch laterally), or at least a few light scales. These blotches narrow laterally and often continue to the venter as a thin irregular dark bar. The nose, from above the eyes to the tip, is suffused with dark pigment. A broad diagonal dark bar extends from the crown, through the eye, to the angle of the mouth. It is bordered anteriorly by a broad, rather well-defined light bar, and posteriorly by a more poorly defined light bar. The tail is black.

In central and western New Mexico, the ground color may be rather similar, but somewhat more intense than that of specimens from Texas.

Arizona specimens may have a grayish or gray green ground color, or may be a greenish yellow to deep gold. The light dorsal areas of yellow specimens are also correspondingly brighter.

Examples from the Harquahala Mountains (central western Arizona) may have black only on the tail, being otherwise patterned in gray green and yellow green, with a light nose.

Neonates of Texas specimens are rather similar to the adults, but a degree of barring is visible on the tail. Neonates of the yellow Arizona examples tend to be paler than the adults, but barring is still visible on the tail.

Similar species: The (usually) dark nose, black tail, and light-spotted dark blotches present a diagnostic suite of characteristics.

Comments: This is a large rattlesnake with a dangerously toxic venom, but many black-tailed rattlesnakes are quiet and disinclined to strike unless seriously threatened or injured. Others, if startled, may immediately swing into a striking coil, with neck high and head lower, hiss, and strike if approached. Parturition has occurred in late July, throughout August, and in early September. Clutches have contained 3–16 neonates, with 4–9 being the norm. Neonates often remain with the mother for a week or more.

ADDITIONAL SUBSPECIES

Other subspecies occur in Mexico.

132. Twin-spotted Rattlesnake

Crotalus pricei pricei

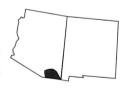

Abundance/Range: This is a moderately common rattlesnake of specialized habitats. In the United States this little rattlesnake is restricted in distribution to subsummit and summit areas of the rugged Pinaleno, Huachuca, Santa Rita, Graham, Dos Cabezas, and Chiricahua mountains in the southeastern corner of Arizona. From this restricted U.S. range, it occurs in the Sierra Madre Occidental mountains at least as far south as southern Durango, Mexico.

Habitat: The lowest elevation at which this species is known to occur in Arizona is about 6,200 feet. From this it ranges upward to 10,700 feet. It

Twin-spotted Rattlesnake

is a species well adapted to life in rocky montane meadows, fissured out-croppings, and extensive slopes of talus.

Size: Although this diminutive rattlesnake is known to attain 26 inches in length, most seen are between 12 and 18 inches. The 1–8 neonates are between 6 and 8 inches in length.

Identifying features: This is a small, slender rattlesnake with a relatively narrow head and a small rattle. It has grayish ground color (occasionally with the vaguest blush of pink dorsally) and paired dark paravertebral spots, sometimes connected dorsally to form a short, dumbbell-shaped blotch. A nearly horizontal, dark postorbital marking is often present. The crown of the head may bear several dark spots, and the banded tail is yellowish at the tip. Neonates are so dark that their dorsal markings are largely obscured.

Similar snakes: None.

Comments: Without a concerted effort to find it, this is not a rattlesnake that one would normally encounter. However, hikers and campers traversing the snake's Sky Island home do occasionally happen across one or more.

This is one of the several montane rattlesnakes that would be discovered far less frequently if it were not so prone to rattle. These snakes are often encountered coiled quietly in patches of sun along hiking paths, or basking atop talus following a summer rain. In midsummer, 2–9 babies are born, coinciding with the birth of mountain spiny lizards (*Sceloporus jarrovi*), a prey species. It is not known whether the twin-spot is an annual, biennial, or triennial breeder in the coolness of its mountain homelands.

ADDITIONAL SUBSPECIES

There are Mexican subspecies, but none in the United States.

133. Red Diamond Rattlesnake

Crotalus ruber

Abundance/Range: The red diamond rattlesnake can be relatively common in areas of prime habitat. Despite decades of persecution in San Diego County, California, it continues to persist in the vicinity of some of the smaller cities and is actually common in some outlying areas. In the United States the range of this Baja species extends only into southwestern California.

Habitat: Boulder-strewn grasslands, aridland scrub, thick chaparral, and open oak and pine woodlands are among the habitats utilized by this impressive and pretty rattlesnake. It is also occasionally encountered in agricultural districts, especially if bordered by undeveloped land. This snake may occur at up to 5,000 feet in elevation.

Size: This is a large and heavy-bodied rattlesnake. While those seen are

Red Diamond Rattlesnake

Red Diamond Rattlesnake

typically between 2 and 4½ feet in length, occasional examples attain 5 feet in length. The largest recorded specimen was 5 feet 5 inches long. Five to 12 (rarely to 20) young are born in a clutch. Neonates are about 1 foot in length.

Identifying features: Although variable in ground color and pattern, the reddest red diamond rattlesnakes are beautiful animals indeed. From what has come to be thought of as the typical red coloration, this snake grades downward through pink to a rather dull reddish tan. The diamonds are also variable in intensity and definition. Even on those specimens with the best-defined, white-outlined diamonds, these markings are paler anteriorly and posteriorly than at midbody. Some snakes have the diamonds defined only on the anterior and posterior margins, with the lateral areas merging almost imperceptibly with the lateral ground color. The tail is boldly ringed with black and white. A light diagonal preocular and postocular line is present. The first lower labial is divided (do not try to check this on a living snake). Neonates are much duller than the adults, often exhibiting a ground color of gray. This usually becomes suffused with red after only a shed or two. The keeled scales are in 29 rows and the anal plate is undivided.

Similar species: Red-phase western diamond-backs can closely resemble the color of the red diamond rattlesnake; however, the ranges of the two species barely abut (and do not overlap).

Comments: This spectacular rattlesnake is usually quiet, nonrattling, and nonaggressive. However, the occasional aggressive specimen will quickly assume an impressively hostile striking position, neck held in a high loop, lowered head facing its antagonist. Male-to-male combat is well documented. This rattlesnake occasionally partially ascends trees or shrubs, or may lie atop thick vertical grasses a foot or two above the ground.

ADDITIONAL SUBSPECIES

None.

134. Mojave Rattlesnake
Crotalus scutulatus scutulatus

Abundance/Range: The Mojave rattlesnake is a relatively common species, but in many areas its true population statistics are skewed because it is often mistaken for the even more abundant, and often sympatric, western diamond-back. From its Mexican stronghold, this rattler ranges northward into western Texas and immediately adjacent south central New Mexico. The range then dips south of the border, turning northward again into south-western New Mexico, much of Arizona, southern Nevada, and southern California. Reports of it occurring in San Diego County, California, are rampant but not yet verified.

Habitat: This rattlesnake is essentially a species of rock-strewn grass-lands, desert scrub areas, sparsely vegetated valleys, creosote-bush flats, and rocky, vegetated mountain slopes. Plant communities with which it is associated include mesquite, Joshua tree, cholla and prickly pear, and creosote bush. It has been found at elevations of 8,300 feet.

Size: Although dangerous, the Mojave rattlesnake is not as imposing as some other species. Most seen are in the 18–40-inch range, and the largest recorded specimen measured only 51 inches long. A clutch can contain 2–13 neonates that are about 10½ inches long.

Mojave Rattlesnake

Identifying features: Because of the irregular, very well defined, dark diamond- or rhomboid-shaped markings on its back, the Mojave rattlesnake was long referred to as the Mojave diamond-back. The dorsal markings have light centers and are usually rather broadly margined with dark brown pigment. The ground color may vary from greenish yellow, through tan, to brownish or olive. Of the two rows of lateral blotches, the uppermost is only faintly defined, but the lower row contrasts strongly with the ground color. There are two light diagonal facial stripes. The aft stripe passes downward behind the angle of the jaws. The tail is ringed, the dark rings being irregular, often offset vertebrally, and less than half as wide as the white to light gray ones.

Except in the western Texas–southeastern New Mexico population, where the head scales are very apt to be fragmented, the Mojave rattlesnake has a characteristic crown scalation. There are usually 2 or 3 rather large scales between the supraoculars, followed by numerous crown scales that are proportionately larger than those on the heads of all rattlesnakes other than those in the genus *Sistrurus*. Neonates are very similar to the adults in appearance. The scales are in 25 rows and the anal plate is undivided.

Similar species: The western diamond-back has well-defined black and white tail rings of equal width. The red diamond rattlesnake also has a more precise coontail pattern, and even the duller examples have a redder ground color than the Mojave.

Comments: Despite its ability to put on a very impressive defensive display, the Mojave is often a quiet rattlesnake that would rather avoid than confront a threat. When frightened, it often lowers (rather than elevates) its head and raises its tail, which is then flicked slowly from side to side, producing a very minimal, but quite audible, "tick-tick-ticking" sound. However, once enraged, *C. s. scutulatus* can become an animated and formidable adversary, rattling loudly, and striking with such force that its entire body may slide forward.

This snake species spends considerable periods in the unused burrows of small mammals, and does not, apparently, congregate in any great numbers to hibernate.

Because of its superficially similar pattern and coloration, the Mojave rattlesnake is often confused with the western diamond-backed rattlesnake.

The potent neurotoxic property of the venom of this rattlesnake is legend—but the legend is not always deserved. In reality, the venom is populationally variable, being extremely virulent and highly neurotoxic in some regions, and largely without neurotoxic properties in other regions. The neurotoxin is identifiable, and is now called Mojave-toxin.

ADDITIONAL SUBSPECIES

There are Mexican subspecies.

135. Tiger Rattlesnake

Crotalus tigris

Abundance/Range: Although seemingly not present in any great concentrations, the tiger rattlesnake is not considered a rare species. The range of this small but impressive rattlesnake is centered in the Sonoran Desert and extends northward from southern Sonora, Mexico, to south central Arizona.

Habitat: The tiger rattlesnake is a species of rocky hillsides, canyons, escarpments, outcroppings, desert washes, and cliff-faces in thornscrub

Tiger Rattlesnake

Tiger Rattlesnake

desert. Plant associations include saguaro-ocotillo, as well as mesquite-creosote bush. The snake seldom roams far from rocky terrain. It occurs upward on some rock-strewn, vegetated desert slopes to the lowest level of the evergreen hardwoods (about 4,800 feet).

Size: This is a rather small but heavy-bodied rattlesnake. Most seen are between 18 and 26 inches in length, but occasional males near or attain 36 inches. Clutch size ranges from 1 to 6, with 2–4 (often 3) being the normal number. Neonates are about 9 inches long.

Identifying features: A small head, a heavy body, and a proportionately huge rattle typify this interesting and variably colored rattlesnake. The ground color varies from almost black, through gray to buff, yellow, and pinkish orange. The bands, which are most prominently dorsally, are gray through brown to lava black, and extend from neck to tailtip. The head may be either vaguely patterned or unpatterned. The scales are keeled and in 23 rows. The anal plate is undivided.

Similar species: The southwestern speckled rattlesnake has a proportionately larger head and a row of small scales between the rostral and the prenasal scales.

Comments: It has been suggested that the very small head of this snake is an adaptation that allows the extraction of immobilized, envenomated prey from narrow crevices in the rocky escarpments and canyonsides that this snake inhabits.

Studies indicate that the tiger rattlesnake has a very toxic venom (containing a high percentage of neurotoxins) but, because of its small head, a relatively low venom yield. Despite the low yield, this rattlesnake should be treated with great respect and caution.

ADDITIONAL SUBSPECIES

None.

SPECKLED RATTLESNAKE COMPLEX

Taxonomic note: Until 2007, the Panamint rattlesnake was considered a subspecies of *Crotalus mitchelli*.

136. Southwestern Speckled Rattlesnake

Crotalus mitchellii pyrrhus

Abundance/Range: This rattlesnake can be relatively abundant in rocky desert habitats. Because of its nearly perfect camouflage, unless it is moving or rattling, it can be easily overlooked.

This snake ranges northward from southern Baja California and northern Sonora to the vicinity of Riverside County, California, extreme southern Nevada, southwestern Utah, and western Arizona.

Habitat: Rock- and boulder-strewn areas are favored habitats of this arid-land rattlesnake. It occurs most often in open, sparsely vegetated desert. Look for it also near the sides of buttes and mesas, and near desert outcroppings and escarpments at elevations up to 8,000 feet.

Size: This rattlesnake attains 2–4 feet in length. The head is rather small, but body girth is considerable. Neonates are between 8½ and 10½ inches in length.

Identifying features: The southwestern speckled rattlesnake displays a great variety of ground colors and a far less precise pattern than most

Southwestern Speckled Rattlesnake

Southwestern Speckled Rattlesnake

rattlesnakes. In fact, it is the most variable and intricately colored of the rattlesnakes of the United States.

The ground color may vary from off-white to yellowish, from tan to gray, or from pinkish to orange. The darker crossbands are hazy and have imprecise edges. Speckles of dark pigment in the light areas, and vice versa, are the norm in this race. Some individuals from regions of dark rocks and/or ancient lava beds may be almost black. The tail is usually rather conspicuously banded, and darkest near the tip. A light triangle, bordered by a darker bar fore and aft, is usually present beneath each eye. The supraocular scales are not wrinkled, and there is a row of small scales separating the prenasals from the rostral scale. Neonates look pretty much like the adults, but may be just a bit more precisely patterned.

Similar species: Sidewinders move in a characteristic mode, oblique to the direction in which their head is pointing. They also have raised supraoculars ("horns"). Western diamond-backs have a coon's tail of black and white rings. Mojave rattlers have enlarged scales on top of the head and a black and gray ringed tail. The southern Pacific and the northern Pacific rattlesnakes tend to have distinctly diamond-shaped dorsal blotches at midbody. Tiger rattlesnakes are less distinctly speckled, and no small scales separate the prenasals from the rostral.

Comments: During the summer months, speckled rattlesnakes often utilize the unused burrows of ground squirrels or kangaroo rats, or the middens of wood rats for seclusion.

This rattlesnake has a formidably potent venom and often a nervous, ready-to-bite demeanor. It should be studiously avoided.

Clutches contain 2–11 neonates, but normally 3–8 are produced.

ADDITIONAL SUBSPECIES

None in the United States.

137. Panamint Rattlesnake

Crotalus stephensi

Abundance/Range: This fairly common rattlesnake occurs in eastern central California and southwestern Nevada. Because of their solitary and secretive summer habits and camouflage coloration, Panamint rattlesnakes are often thought to be uncommon when this is not actually the case. A better idea of area populations can often be gotten in the autumn, when the snakes gather at traditional denning sites—fissured escarpments and ledges, abandoned mines, caves, and other such settings. At some dens, 20, 50, or even more snakes will congregate.

Habitat: The Panamint rattlesnake is associated primarily with rocky, aridland foothill, escarpment, and outcropping habitats, but may also be encountered in sandy creosote bush and cactus-studded desert settings, and even in open coniferous woodlands. It is often seen crossing desert roadways in the early to late evening. The Panamint rattler ranges upward to nearly 8,000 feet in elevation.

Size: This rattler is adult at 26–36 inches (rarely slightly longer) in length. Neonates average 10 inches in length.

Identifying features: This is a rather small-headed, heavy-bodied, large-rattled rattlesnake that can be difficult to positively identify. The ground

Panamint Rattlesnake

color of this interesting rattlesnake is variable, tending to blend well with the color of the substrate on which the snake dwells. The ground color is usually buff, tan, reddish, brown, or grayish, and the darker markings, which are usually rather well defined and margined with lighter pigment, may be in the form of bands or diamonds. The head often lacks any well-defined pattern, but may bear a diffuse, gray or tan, diagonally oriented, subocular triangle. The dorsal surface of the supraocular scales is often greaved (puckered), pitted, or has weakly uneven outer edges. The pre-nasal and rostral scales are in contact (not separated from each other by small scales). The tail is narrowly but evenly and distinctly banded and blackens distally, and the dark color also encompasses the basal rattle segment. Neonates are very similar to the adults, but may be somewhat more precisely marked. There are 23–27 rows of keeled scales, and the anal plate is not divided.

This snake varies somewhat in temperament, some specimens lying quietly until actually prodded, while others will assume a striking coil and rattle loudly while a disturbing object is still some distance away.

Similar species: See the southwestern speckled rattlesnake, account 136.

ADDITIONAL SUBSPECIES

None.

THE WESTERN RATTLESNAKE COMPLEX

This group of rattlers is in taxonomic disarray. All were traditionally considered subspecies of the prairie rattlesnake, *Crotalus viridis*.

Based on results of two DNA analyses, some authorities feel that six of the forms are subspecies of the northern Pacific rattlesnake, *Crotalus oreganus*, and two, the prairie and the Hopi rattlesnakes, are races of *C. viridis*. Others consider the Hopi rattlesnake to be merely a dwarfed variant of the prairie rattlesnake, the Arizona black rattler to be a full species, and *C. oreganus* to comprise five subspecies (we have adopted this outlook herein). Still others, having apparently a philosophical dislike of the subspecies concept, consider all eight forms to be full species.

Most examples of all these snakes bear prominent dorsal saddles that are especially distinct on young individuals. On some, however, the markings are bars rather than saddles. The scales are usually in 25 (23–27) rows. There are usually more than 2 internasal scales touching the rostral scale. There are two variably distinct light facial stripes. The posterior (postocular) stripe passes *above* the corner of the mouth.

138. Arizona Black Rattlesnake

Crotalus cerberus

Abundance/Range: This rattlesnake is found from northwestern Arizona, southeastward to western New Mexico. It is a secretive but not uncommon form.

Habitat: This interesting rattlesnake occurs in habitats as diverse as montane forest, woodland, and upland desert chaparral. Altitudinal preferences range from 3,500 to 9,150 feet.

Size: Adults are of moderate size, attaining 28–36 inches. Occasional specimens may reach a length of 42 inches. From 3 to 15 (normally 4–9) neonates, measuring about 10½ inches in length, are produced.

Identifying features: This, the darkest of the western rattlesnake group, is capable of considerable day to nighttime color change (metachrosis). By day, the snakes are the darkest with some being an almost overall jet black. The very broad blotches are narrowly outlined with cream or yellow. The ground color of the same snake may lighten to olive gray or blackish gray by night, at which time the light-outlined, darker blotches are readily

Arizona Black Rattlesnake

Arizona Black Rattlesnake

visible. Other examples are lighter, varying from a dark-blotched, rather light gray to brownish gray. The blotches are best defined on the posterior two thirds of the body. The facial pattern of a diagonal, light preorbital and postorbital bar may be rather strongly apparent or, as is often the case, virtually indiscernible. Narrow light bands are visible on the tail of light-colored examples. Neonates, which number 3–12 (usually 5–8), and are about 10 inches in length, are much lighter and more boldly patterned than even the lightest colored adults.

Although dangerously venomous, it tends to be less irascible than many other forms of the western rattlesnake complex.

Similar species: Also see the accounts for the prairie rattlesnake (144) and the Grand Canyon rattlesnake (140).

ADDITIONAL SUBSPECIES

As currently described, none.

139. Northern Pacific Rattlesnake

Crotalus oreganus oreganus

Abundance/Range: This is an abundant snake throughout most of its range. It can persist in rural and suburban locales if sufficient cover is present. This, the northwestern representative of the species, occurs southward from south central British Columbia to central western Idaho and central California.

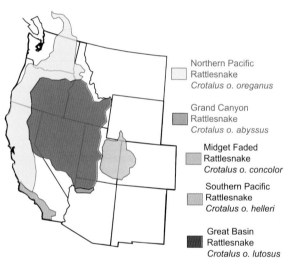

Northern Pacific
Rattlesnake
Crotalus o. oreganus

Grand Canyon
Rattlesnake
Crotalus o. abyssus

Midget Faded
Rattlesnake
Crotalus o. concolor

Southern Pacific
Rattlesnake
Crotalus o. helleri

Great Basin
Rattlesnake
Crotalus o. lutosus

Because of prevailing cool temperatures, it is largely diurnal in habits, but on hot evenings may remain active until well after dark.

Habitat: Rocky ledges, escarpments, and outcroppings in pasturelands and grasslands are favored sites. Rocky hillsides usually also provide ideal habitat. It is able to survive in comparatively austere surroundings up to about 8,000 feet in elevation if it can access the burrows of ground squirrels or other small mammals.

Size: This snake occasionally attains 5 feet in length, but is usually only 3½–4 feet long when adult. From 3 to 15 (normally 4–9) neonates, measuring about 10½ inches in length, are produced.

Northern Pacific Rattlesnake

Northern Pacific Rattlesnake

Identifying features: The northern Pacific rattlesnake is strongly and precisely patterned when young, but the pattern tends to become more diffuse with advancing age. Although some adults can be strongly melanistic, most retain greenish brown to grayish brown sides and dorsal ground color. The dorsal markings are in the form of broad, well-defined (sometimes diamond-shaped) blotches on the anterior two thirds of the snake, but in the form of dark bars posteriorly. The tail is strongly barred, but the terminal dark bar is not noticeably wider than those that precede it. The light facial stripes may be well defined or obscure, and the top of the head is not usually boldly patterned. The northern Pacific rattler probably does not breed any more often than every second year at the southern extreme of its range, and may reproduce only every third or fourth year in more northerly, or normally cold, regions.

Similar species: The more easterly prairie rattlesnake (account 144) is of very similar appearance; however, the ranges do not overlap.

Comments: This snake may either rattle furiously or lie quietly when approached. However, most that we have approached were quite defensive.

ADDITIONAL SUBSPECIES

140. The Grand Canyon Rattlesnake, *C. o. abyssus*, attains a length of 18–39 inches. Neonates are about 9½ inches in length. This rarely seen subspecies is of restricted distribution, being found only in Arizona's Grand Can-

Grand Canyon Rattlesnake, adult

Grand Canyon Rattlesnake, juvenile

yon and on the north rim. It inhabits pinyon-juniper woodlands as well as desert- and mesquite-scrublands.

This rattlesnake has a faded pattern and a muted ground color. It is capable of limited color change. The ground color of this pretty rattler is often of some shade of pink, but may vary from nearly cream to salmon. The ground color is lightest dorsally. The darker, narrow, sometimes hourglass-shaped dorsal blotches, often barely visible and occasionally absent, are best defined on their anterior and posterior edges. On the sides, the blotches often blend almost imperceptibly with the lateral ground color. The ventrolateral blotches are usually visible but lack a light border. The head is weakly patterned, but vestiges of a diagonal preocular and a postocular stripe may remain. Neonates are much more strongly patterned than the adults. The tail is banded, most distinctly distally. The basal segment of the rattle is dark (often black).

141. The Midget Faded Rattlesnake, *C. o. concolor*, is quite similar in appearance to the Grand Canyon rattler, but is clad in scales of sandstone orange, tan, cream, or yellow brown. The darker dorsal blotches are relatively broad and may be well defined to virtually indiscernible. If present, the dorsal blotches may be defined by darker pigment along their anterior and posterior margins. The dorsal surface of the head is largely unpatterned, and the two typical facial stripes are obscure. The basal seg-

Midget Faded Rattlesnake

ment of the rattle is dark. Neonate midget faded rattlesnakes are about 7½ inches in length, number 2–10 (normally 3–6) in each clutch, and are more prominently patterned than the adult snakes. In drop for drop toxicity, the venom of this race surpasses that of other subspecies. Despite its small size (18–24 inches, rarely a little more) the midget faded rattlesnake, which can be moderately aggressive, should be considered a dangerously venomous snake. This race ranges in suitable rocky desert and plains habitats over much of eastern Utah, immediately adjacent southwestern Wyoming, and western Colorado. It is considered uncommon by many researchers.

142. The Southern Pacific Rattlesnake, *C. o. helleri*, is one of the larger races of western rattlesnake. Adult at 30–44 inches, occasional specimens may attain a length of 54 inches. This southern California and Baja race has a brown to olive brown ground color and deeper brown, dorsal blotches that are most prominent and often diamond shaped at midbody, where they are completely outlined by light (cream to yellowish) pigment. The blotches are more obscure and less precisely outlined anteriorly, and there are narrow to dark bars on the posterior fifth or so of the body. The two light facial markings are diffuse, and may do little more than outline the dark suborbital triangle between them. The tail is ringed, and the terminal dark tail-ring is more than twice the width of the more anterior rings. This

Southern Pacific Rattlesnake

attractive and moderately aggressive rattlesnake is pretty much a habitat generalist. It may be encountered in areas as diverse as seaside habitats, grassy plains, scrubby deserts, rocky hillsides, agricultural areas, and open woodlands. Neonates average about 10 inches in length, number 3–14 per clutch, and are vividly patterned.

143. The Great Basin Rattlesnake, *C. o. lutosus*, has an extensive range. From northwestern California, it ranges eastward and northward to western Utah, southern Wyoming, and southeastern Oregon. Rocky hillsides, buttes, and mesas, grassy plains, meadows, barren alkali flats, and agricultural areas are all inhabited by this abundant, 3–4-foot-long snake.

The Great Basin rattler has an ash gray, tan, yellowish, or buff ground color. The dorsal pattern consists of rather narrow, well-separated, usually light-centered, and sometimes light-edged, deep brown saddles. These narrow to bars posteriorly. The tail is barred, and the terminal dark bar is very wide and often almost black in color. The two light facial stripes vary from well defined to virtually nonexistent. When the snake is young, the top of the head bears an intricate pattern of dark blotching separated by light lines, and a light line from eye to eye. This patterning diffuses with advancing age. Females produce young biennially or triennially, depend-

Great Basin Rattlesnake

ing on how fast they can replace their body fat content. The precisely patterned neonates number between 3 and 14 (normally 5–8) per clutch, and are about 10 inches in total length.

144. Prairie Rattlesnake

Crotalus viridis viridis

Abundance/Range: This irascible snake is abundant throughout much of its range. It is the easternmost representative of the complex. It ranges southward from southeastern Alberta and adjacent Saskatchewan to southern Texas and northern Mexico. It may be found from sea level to elevations of about 8,000 feet.

Habitat: The prairie rattler is a grassland-prairie race that has been extirpated in populated areas but persists in some numbers elsewhere. It may be common in arroyos, in canyons, and along debris-strewn washes. It is also associated with prairie dog towns and ground squirrel colonies, where it uses the rodents' burrows and preys on the young. The prairie rattlesnake hibernates in rocky outcroppings, escarpments, and mountainside dens.

Size: This rattler attains a length of more than 4½ feet, but is sexually mature at as little as 2½ feet in length. Neonates are 10 inches long.

Identifying features: The specific name refers to the greenish ground color of some examples, but the ground color may also be brownish or grayish (please also see comments below on the Hopi rattlesnake variant). The dorsal markings are blotches anteriorly and bars posteriorly. They are usually well separated and well defined. The blotches on the anterior two thirds of the body are edged anteriorly and posteriorly with darker pigment, and are completely margined with light pigment. Posterior blotches are less well defined. The two light facial stripes are usually well defined, and a light bar crosses the dorsal surface of the head from supraocular scale to supraocular scale. The tail is strongly but narrowly barred, and the distalmost bar and basal segment of rattle are black. Neonates are more precisely patterned than adults.

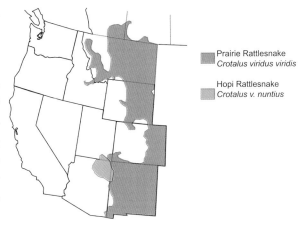

Prairie Rattlesnake
Crotalus viridus viridis

Hopi Rattlesnake
Crotalus v. nuntius

Prairie Rattlesnake

Reproduction probably occurs no more frequently than biennially in the south, and only every third or fourth year in the north. The clutch can number from 3 to 21 babies, but is normally between 6 and 12 in number.

Comments: Temperatures dictate the activity periods of this rattlesnake. It is diurnal much of the time, but crepuscular and nocturnal when warm temperatures permit. Contrary to popular belief, the prairie rattler probably does not cohabit peacefully with prairie dogs, burrowing owls, or other endotherms. Rather, is seeks solace in the burrows, and the burrow makers are known to be on the list of prey species.

PROBLEMATIC VARIANT

144a. The prairie rattlesnake variant known as the Hopi Rattlesnake was long designated as *Crotalus viridis nuntius*. It is currently considered merely a dwarfed variant of the prairie rattlesnake. This rather slender snake is adult at 18–24 inches in length, but may occasionally attain 27 inches. Neonates are about 7 inches in length and number 3–10 in a litter.

The Hopi variant occurs in northeastern Arizona and immediately adjacent areas of Utah and New Mexico. It is associated with arid and

Hopi Rattlesnake phase

semiarid plains and grasslands, but it may be encountered in open coniferous woodlands as well. This rattlesnake is diurnal in the spring, but as temperatures warm, becomes more crepuscular and nocturnal.

The ground color of this snake varies from reddish gray, reddish brown, pink, or pale orange and metachrosis (day to night color changes) can be dramatic. The dorsal markings are widest anteriorly, in the form of light-margined, well-defined blotches or wide bars centrally, but are paler, less prominent, and lack light edging posteriorly. The tail is barred; the basal rattle segment is black. The facial stripes are well defined; the anterior bars and dark suborbital marking often meet on top of the snout. Posteriorly, the dorsal surface of the head tends to be entirely or largely unpatterned.

The Hopi rattler figures prominently in the ceremonial dances of the Hopi (and other) Indians. Tribal members handle this venomous snake with relative impunity. Nonetheless, remember that this snake can be short tempered and is capable of producing serious envenomation. It should be considered dangerous.

The Hopi rattler tends to feed largely on lizards, a prey item lacking the potential to replace the snake's body fat quickly. Because of this, female Hopi rattlesnakes probably reproduce either biennially or triennially.

Ridge-nosed Rattlesnakes

145. Arizona Ridge-nosed Rattlesnake

Crotalus willardi willardi

Abundance/Range: This is a locally distributed rattlesnake of the canyons of the Santa Rita, Patagonia, and Huachuca mountains of southeastern Arizona and the northernmost peaks of the Sierra Madre Occidental of Sonora, Mexico. There is a possibility that this rattlesnake also occurs in Arizona's Chiricahua Mountains, but this has not yet been confirmed. It may be found at 5,000–9,000 feet in elevation.

Arizona Ridge-nosed Rattlesnake
Crotalus w. willardi

New Mexican Ridge-nosed Rattlesnake
Crotalus willardus obscurus

Habitat: Canyon stream bottoms and associated rocky, grassed, sparsely wooded canyon slopes are the habitats of this rattlesnake. It is often found partially concealed in leaf litter along trails.

Arizona Ridge-nosed Rattlesnake

Size: This snake seldom exceeds 20 inches in total length. The record length is 25½ inches. Neonates are about 7½ inches long.

Identifying features: This rattlesnake is clad in attractive, crisp colors that blend well with the fallen leaves of its montane homelands. The ground color is russet, and the dorsal cross-barring is a very light gray, bordered along the front and the back by darker reddish brown pigment. The face is prominently striped with white, and a vertical white bar appears on the rostral scale. The tail is grayish with russet dorsal striping. Neonates are grayer than the adults and often have a yellow orange tail for the first few weeks of their life. The scales are keeled, usually in 23–27 rows, and the anal plate is not divided.

Similar species: None in Arizona. The facial markings and rattle are diagnostic.

Comments: Breeding occurs in late spring and possibly in late autumn. Parturition occurs in August and early September. From 1 to 9 babies are born, with 2–5 seeming to be the norm. Babies indulge in caudal luring, continuing to utilize this method of prey procurement even after the tail color fades.

New Mexican Ridge-nosed Rattlesnake

ADDITIONAL SUBSPECIES

146. The New Mexican Ridge-nosed Rattlesnake, *C. w. obscurus*, is one of the smallest of the rattlesnakes. Adults are normally 16–20 inches in length, and only rarely is a length of 24 inches attained. It occurs in montane meadows, at streamside in canyons, and in open pine-fir-oak woodlands of the Animas and the Peloncillo mountains of extreme southwestern New Mexico and Arizona. It is also found in the Sierra San Luis of Chihuahua, Mexico.

Adults are grayish to reddish gray snakes, with a peppered appearance and faint, but apparent, dorsal barring. The barring is somewhat lighter than the ground color, and margined fore and aft with darker gray pigment. A prominent ridge follows the dorsal contour of the snout. Facial markings are obscure or absent. There are two rows of lateral spots, both equally obscure. The gray tail bears a dorsal stripe. Neonates are brown to reddish brown, have light lips, and usually a dark tail.

This is a federally threatened and state-endangered rattlesnake.

Massasaugas and Pygmy Rattlesnakes

There are only two species in this genus, and only one, the desert massas-auga, occurs in the west. Rather than the fragmented crown scales borne by the rattlesnakes of the genus *Crotalus*, the snakes of the genus *Sistrurus* have 9 large scales (similar to those of most harmless snakes) on top of the head. Massasaugas have a relatively slender tail and a small rattle that can be difficult to hear.

This is a nervous little snake that will not hesitate to bite if provoked. In drop-for-drop potency, the venom is quite toxic. However, the venom yield is relatively low. Despite this the massasauga should be considered a dangerously venomous species and treated with respect and caution. These snakes are largely nocturnal and are particularly active during the summer rains.

Parturition occurs in mid to late summer. Brood size varies from 2 to about 10 babies (3–6 is normal). Neonates are a slender 6½–7 inches in length.

147. Desert Massasauga

Sistrurus catenatus edwardsi

Abundance/Range: Although there are some ar-eas where the desert massasauga is relatively com-mon, over much of its range it is uncommon to rare. The range of this little rattlesnake extends westward from southern and central Texas to the little remaining grassland habitat in the extreme southeastern corner of Arizona. It also occurs in immediately adjacent areas south of the interna-
tional boundary in Mexico. It may be found from sea level to an altitude of about 6,900 feet.

Habitat: This is an arid-grassland species, but where the grasslands have been destroyed, it continues to persist (at least temporarily) in marginally suitable opuntia-agave habitats. It has been eradicated from many historic sites by agricultural development.

Size: This, the smallest of the three races of the massasauga, is adult at 14–18 inches. The largest documented size of this relatively slender snake is about 22½ inches. Neonates are about 7½ inches long.

Identifying features: The desert massasauga is a pretty but quietly colored little snake. Eastern examples tend to be a little more deeply colored than the pale specimens from the Cochise County, Arizona grasslands. The ground color is a sandy tan that usually blends well with the substrate on which the snake is found. There are about 35 (27–41) dorsal saddles of darker brown (sometimes with an orangish blush) that are narrowly edged with even darker pigment. A dark diagonal eye stripe (often the darkest marking on the snake) covers most of each cheek and extends upward over the snout anterior to the eye. On the face, this is bordered both above and below by a narrow white line. An irregular elongate bar, beginning on each supraocular, extends back onto the nape. The tail is prominently banded. The scales are keeled, usually in 23 rows, and the anal plate is undivided.

Similar species: Although similarly sized, the twin-spotted rattlesnake of southeastern Arizona has twinned dorsal markings, fragmented head scales, and is a montane species. The Great Plains rat snake is quite similar in color, but lacks a rattle.

Comments: Because of habitat degradation (such as overgrazing) the desert massasauga may actually be rapidly declining in some areas. Breeding occurs both in the autumn and in the spring of the year.

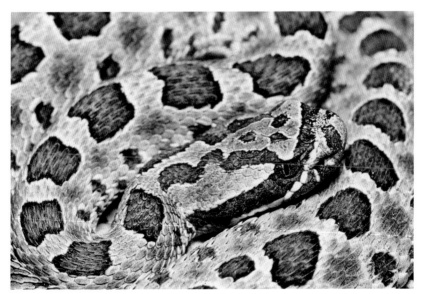

Desert Massasauga

ADDITIONAL SUBSPECIES

Although two additional subspecies are recognized, both occur to the east of the scope of this book.

However, a population of intergrade massasaugas exists in southeastern Colorado. The parent races were the desert (*Sistrurus catenatus edwardsi*) and the western (*Sistrurus catenatus tergeminus*) massasaugas. The snakes in the Colorado population attain an adult size of about 2 feet and bear intermediate characteristics.

Desert x Western Massasauga

Glossary

Aestivation: A period of warm weather inactivity; often triggered by excessive heat or drought.

Ambient temperature: The temperature of the surrounding environment.

Anterior: Toward the front.

Anus: The external opening of the cloaca; the vent.

Arboreal: Tree-dwelling.

Brille: The transparent "spectacle" covering the eyes of a snake.

Brumation: The reptilian equivalent of hibernation.

Caudal: Pertaining to the tail.

Cloaca: The common chamber into which digestive, urinary, and reproductive systems empty and which itself opens exteriorly through the vent or anus.

Constrict: To wrap tightly in coils and squeeze.

Convergent evolution: Evolution of two unrelated species with similar outcome or adaptation as the result of environmental (or other) conditions.

Cornified: Keratinized, horny.

Crepuscular: Active at dusk and/or dawn.

Deposition: As used here, the laying of eggs or birthing of young.

Deposition site: The spot chosen by the female to lay her eggs or have young.

Dimorphic: A difference in form, build, or coloration within the same species; often sex linked.

Diurnal: Active in the daytime.

Dorsal: Pertaining to the back; upper surface.

Dorsolateral: Pertaining to the upper sides.

Dorsum: The upper surface.

Ecological niche: The precise habitat utilized by a species.

Ectothermic: "Cold blooded"; body heat absorbed from the environment.

Endothermic: "Warm blooded"; produces own body heat.

Form: An identifiable species or subspecies.

Fossorial: Adapted for burrowing. Pertaining to a burrowing species.

Genus, pl. genera: A taxonomic classification of a group of species having similar characteristics. The genus falls between the next higher designation of "family" and the next lower designation of "species." The genus name is always capitalized when written.

Glottis: The opening of the windpipe in the mouth.

Gravid: The reptilian equivalent of mammalian pregnancy.

Gular: Pertaining to the throat.

Heliothermic: Pertaining to a species that basks in the sun to thermoregulate.

Hemipenes: The dual copulatory organs of male lizards and snakes.

Hemipenis: The singular of hemipenes.

Herpetology: The study (often scientifically oriented) of reptiles and amphibians.

Hibernacula: Winter dens.

Hybrid: Offspring resulting from the breeding of two species.

Insular: As used here, island-dwelling.

Intergrade: Offspring resulting from the breeding of two subspecies.

Internasals: A pair of scales on the snout immediately posterior to, and usually in contact with, the rostral scale.

Jacobson's organs: Highly enervated olfactory pits in the palate of snakes and lizards.

Juvenile: A young or immature specimen.

Keel: As used here, a ridge along the center of a scale.

Labial: Pertaining to the lips.

Lateral: Pertaining to the side.

Melanism: A profusion of black pigment.

Mental: The scale at the tip of the lower lip.

Metachrosis: The changing of color, often in response to climatic conditions or to photoperiod.

Middorsal: Pertaining to the middle of the back.

Midventral: Pertaining to the center of the belly or abdomen.

Monotypic: Containing but one type.

Nocturnal: Active at night.

Ontogenetic: Age-related (color) changes.

Oviparous: Reproducing by means of eggs that hatch after laying.

Ovoviviparous: Reproducing by means of shelled or membrane-contained eggs that hatch prior to, or at deposition.

Photoperiod: The daily/seasonally variable length of the hours of daylight.

Postocular: To the rear of the eye.

Race: A subspecies.

Rostral: The (often modified) scale on the tip of the snout.

Rugose: Not smooth; wrinkled or tuberculate.

Saxicolous: Rock-dwelling.

Scute: Scale. Usually referring to a large platelike scale, such as the belly scales of most snakes.

Species: A group of similar creatures that produce viable young when breeding. The taxonomic designation that falls beneath genus and above subspecies. Abbreviation, sp.; plural spp.

Suboculars: A row of small scales separating the eye from the labials.

Subspecies: The subdivision of a species. A race that may differ slightly in color, size, scalation, or other criteria. Abbreviation, ssp.

Supralabials: The scales edging the upper lip.

Supraoculars: The (often shieldlike) scales above the eyes.

Sympatric: Occurring together.

Taxonomy: The science of classification of plants and animals.

Terrestrial: Land-dwelling.

Thermoregulate: To regulate (body) temperature by choosing a warmer or cooler environment.

Valvular: Valvelike; able to be voluntarily opened and closed.

Vent: The external opening of the cloaca; the anus.

Venter: The underside of a creature; the belly.

Ventral: Pertaining to the undersurface or belly.

Ventrolateral: Pertaining to the sides of the venter, or belly.

Acknowledgments

Many people helped with the compilation of facts and photos for this book.

Brad Alexander, Robert Applegate, Chris Bednarski, Abe Blank, Jerry Boyer, Tim Burkhardt, Dennis Cathcart, Harold DeLisle, Will Flaxington, Chris Gruenwald, Bob Hansen, Andy Holycross, Fred Gehlbach, Jim Harding, Pierson Hill, Richard Hoyer, Gordy Johnston, Gerald Keown, Ken King, Jason Jones, Jeff Lemm, Randy Limburg, Wendy McKeown, Josh McLane, Jim Melli, Gerold and Cindy Merker, Dennie Miller, Mitch Mulks, Regis Opferman, Ed Pirog, Gus Rentfro, Mark Robertson, Chris Rombaugh, Buzz Ross, Dan Scolaro, Wade and Emily Sherbrooke, Lorrie Smith, Victor Velasquez, Ernie Wagner, and Anish Yelekar provided field information, companionship and hospitality during our travels.

Randy Babb, Jeff Boundy, Bob Hansen, Richard Hoyer, Paul Moler, Charlie Painter, Mike Souza, J. P. Stephenson, Karl Heinz-Switak, Dale Sylvester, Gerald Sylvester, Tom Tyning, and Wayne Van Devender provided us with field information and help that allowed us to see many southwestern taxa in situ.

Randy Babb, Bob Hansen, Jeff Lemm, and Karl Heinz-Switak also provided us with photographs of taxa that evaded or avoided our field searches.

Chuck Hurt, Craig McIntyre, Bill Love, Chris McQuade, Rob MacInnes, Mike Stuhlman, and Eric Thiss extended to us the privilege of photographing snakes in their respective collections.

Kenny Wray and Gary Nafis were field companions par excellence.

Bibliography

Bartlett, Richard D. 1988. *In Search of Reptiles and Amphibians*. Leiden: E. J. Brill.

Bartlett, Richard D., and Patricia Bartlett. 1999. *Terrarium and Cage Construction and Care*. Hauppauge, N.Y.: Barron's.

Baxter, George T., and Michael D. Stone. 1980. *Amphibians and Reptiles of Wyoming*. Cheyenne: Wyoming Game and Fish Dept.

Behler, John L., and F. Wayne King. 1979. *National Audubon Society Field Guide to North American Reptiles and Amphibians*. New York: Alfred A. Knopf.

Brennan, T. C., and A. T. Holycross. 2006. *A Field Guide to Amphibians and Reptiles in Arizona*. Phoenix: Arizona Game and Fish Department.

———. 2005. *A Field Guide to Amphibians and Reptiles of Maricopa County*. Phoenix: Arizona Game and Fish Department.

Brennan, Thomas C., and M. J. Feldner. 2001. *Lichanura trivirgata trivirgata*. Geographic Distribution. *Herpetological Review* 32(3).

Brown, Philip. 1997. *A Field Guide to Snakes of California*. Houston, Tex.: Gulf Pub.

Brown, Vinson. 1974. *Reptiles and Amphibians of the West*. Happy Camp, Calif.: Naturegraph Pub.

Collins, Joseph T. 1982. *Amphibians and Reptiles in Kansas*. Lawrence: University of Kansas.

Conant, Roger and Joseph T. Collins. 1991. *A Field Guide to Reptiles and Amphibians; Eastern and Central North America*. Boston: Houghton Mifflin Co.

Crother, Brian I., Chair. 2007. Scientific and Standard English Names of Amphibians and Reptiles of North America north of Mexico, with Comments Regarding Confidence in our Understanding. Herpetological Circular 29. St. Louis, Mo.: SSAR.

Degenhardt, William G., Charles W. Painter, and Andrew H. Price. 1996. *Amphibians and Reptiles of New Mexico*. Albuquerque: University of New Mexico Press.

Dowling, Herndon G. 1957. *A Taxonomic Study of the Rat Snakes, Genus* Elaphe *Fitzinger*. V. *The* rosaliae *section*. Ann Arbor: University of Michigan.

———. 1960. A Taxonomic Study of the Rat Snakes, Genus *Elaphe* Fitzinger. VII. The *triaspis* section. *Zoologica* 45: 53–80.

Dowling, Herndon G., and William E. Duellman. 1974–1978. *Systematic Herpetology: A Synopsis of Families and Higher Categories*. New York: HISS Publications.

Dunson, William A., and Gary W. Ehlert. 1971. Effects of Temperature, Salinity, and Surface Water Flow on Distribution of the Sea Snake *Pelamis*. *Limnology and Oceanography* 16(6): 845–853.

Ernst, Carl H. 1992. *Venomous Reptiles of North America*. Washington, D.C.: Smithsonian.

Ernst, Carl H., and Evelyn M. Ernst. 2003. *Snakes of the United States and Canada.* Washington, D.C.: Smithsonian.

Fowlie, Jack A. 1965. *The Snakes of Arizona.* Fallbrook, Calif.: Azul Quinta Press.

Greene, Harry W. 1997. *Snakes, the Evolution of Mystery in Nature.* Berkeley: University of California Press.

Halliday, Tim R., and Kraig Adler (Eds.). 1987. *The Encyclopedia of Reptiles and Amphibians.* New York: Facts on File.

Hammerson, Geoffrey A. 1986. *Amphibians and Reptiles in Colorado.* Denver: Colorado Div. of Wildlife.

Lawson, R., et al. 2005. Phylogeny of the Colubroidea (Serpentes): New Evidence from Mitochondrial and Nuclear Genes. *Molecular Phylogenetics and Evolution* 37: 581–601.

Lemm, Jeffrey M. 2006. *Field Guide to the Amphibians and Reptiles of the San Diego Region.* Berkeley: University of California Press.

Lowe, Charles H., Cecil R. Schwalbe, and Terry B. Johnson. 1986. *The Venomous Reptiles of Arizona.* Phoenix: Arizona Fish and Game Department.

McKeown, Sean. 1996. *A Field Guide to Reptiles and Amphibians in the Hawaiian Islands.* Los Osos, Calif.: Diamond Head Pub.

Mehrtens, John M. 1987. *Living Snakes of the World in Color.* New York: Sterling Pub.

Rossman, Douglas A., Neil B. Ford, and Richard A. Seigel. 1996. *The Garter Snakes: Evolution and Ecology.* Norman: University of Oklahoma Press.

Shaw, Charles E., and Sheldon Campbell. 1974. *Snakes of the American West.* New York: Alfred A. Knopf.

Stebbins, Robert C. 1985. *A Field Guide to Western Reptiles and Amphibians.* Boston: Houghton Mifflin Co.

Storm, Robert M., and William P. Leonard (Eds.). 1995. *Reptiles of Washington and Oregon.* Seattle: Seattle Audubon Soc.

Werner, J. Kirwin, et al. 2004. *Amphibians and Reptiles of Montana.* Missoula, Mont.: Mountain Press.

Wright, Albert H., and A. A. Wright. 1957. *Handbook of Snakes.* Vols. 1 & 2. Ithaca, N.Y.: Comstock.

Some popular and informative Web sites

www.californiaherps.com
www.utahherps.info
www.livingunderworld.org
www.reptilesofaz.com
www.kingsnake.com
www.faunaclassifieds.com
www.caudata.org

Index

R. D. Bartlett is a veteran herpetologist/herpetoculturist with more than forty years' experience in writing, photography, and educating people about reptiles and amphibians. He is the author of numerous books on the subject, including *Guide and Reference to the Snakes of Eastern and Central North America (North of Mexico)* (2005), *Guide and Reference to the Amphibians of Eastern and Central North America (North of Mexico)* (2006), and *Guide and Reference to the Crocodilians, Turtles, and Lizards of Eastern and Central North America (North of Mexico)* (2006). He is the founder of the Reptilian Breeding and Research Institute, a private facility dedicated to herpetofauna study and support.

Patricia P. Bartlett is a biologist/historian who grew up chasing lizards on the mesas in Albuquerque, New Mexico. Had there been Komodo dragons present, she would have chased them, too. She attended Colorado State University with the intention of becoming a veterinarian but found the world of journalism and writing about creatures too interesting to resist. She moved to Florida after graduation, in part because of the reptiles and amphibians found there. Her background includes book editing, magazine production, museum administration, and program administration for a university. She is the author of books on koi, rabbits, and sharks, and has co-authored some 54 titles on natural history and history.